WHY
DIDN'T YOU COME
SOONER?

Stories from my life as a missionary in the Philippines

In a day of short-term commitments, these stories bring a needed emphasis on a life-long calling to become so immersed in another culture and language that its people are attracted to the One who did that for us all. Along the way there are delightful accounts of danger, stretched faith, and transformed lives.

J. DUDLEY WOODBERRY, Dean Emeritus and Senior Professor of Islamic Studies, School of Intercultural Studies, Fuller Theological Seminary

Veteran missionary Richard Varberg has collected powerful true stories gleaned from his forty years of front-line missionary work in the Philippines. I highly recommend this book to all who are interested in missions, especially for those who are training for the missionary task. It is filled to the brim with keen insights that will help both younger and older missionaries to be more effective in their ministry.

LARRY W. CALDWELL, Ph.D., Academic Dean and Professor of Missions, Asian Theological Seminary, Manila, Philippines

This book stirred my soul. Dick and Elenor Varberg are two of the finest missionaries I have ever known and the way God used them, protected them, is using their children and continuing to multiply their 40 years in the Philippines is phenomenal. I would love to see this book placed in the hands of tens of thousands of youth during the years they are considering their future. Eternity is at stake! I do not know how a person can better invest their life.

BOB RICKER, Pastor and Author, Former President of Baptist General Conference

Jesus told his followers to go into all the world with good news. The stories of going have inspired people since the book of Acts. I'm glad Richard Varberg has added his journey to the story.

JOHN ORTBERG, Pastor and Author, Menlo Park Presbyterian Church

Once I started, I could not stop reading this book of stories told by Dick Varberg. He shares instructive episodes from a forty-year career of advancing the gospel throughout the islands of the Philippines. You'll read of prison threats or worse, of dreams in the night in which Christ spoke directly, of tough-minded negotiations that settled disputes, of architectural and construction ingenuity, of harrowing trips in outrigger canoes, and always the hand of the Lord at work to save, to protect and to guide. Be ready to laugh aloud and to shed tears as you read of courage, hope, and transformation.

LELAND ELIASON, Th.D., Executive Director and Provost, Bethel Seminary of Bethel University

---

Cover from left to right:

Varberg and Miguel Baja talk in front of a house ruined in a typhoon. Baja is the father who asked why the missionaries did not come before his son died, possibly without Christ.

Varberg, with his preferred vehicle, stopped to minister to a man with child in Masbate.

A portion of the 72 converts baptized in one service wait in earnest in the waters of Bituon Beach in Masbate.

RICHARD VARBERG

WHY
DIDN'T YOU COME
SOONER?

Stories from my life as a missionary in the Philippines

WILLIAM CAREY
LIBRARY

Why didn't you come sooner?
Stories from my life as a missionary in the Philippines
Copyright © 2009 by Richard Varberg

Published by William Carey Library
1605 E. Elizabeth Street
Pasadena, CA 91104
www.missionbooks.org

Francesca Gacho, copyeditor
Hugh Pinder, graphic design

William Carey Library is a ministry of the
U.S. Center for World Mission
Pasadena, CA
www.uscwm.org

20091STCHG500

Library of Congress Cataloging-in-Publication Data

Varberg, Richard, 1932-
  Why didn't you come sooner? : stories from my life as a missionary in the
Philippines / By Richard Varberg.
    p. cm.
  ISBN 978-0-87808-004-5 (pbk.)
  1. Varberg, Richard, 1932- 2. Missionaries--United States--Biography. 3.
Missionaries--Philippines--Biography. 4. Missions--Philippines. 5.
Baptists--Missions--Philippines. I. Title.
  BV3382.V37A3 2008
  266'.65092--dc22
  [B]
                          2008014500

DEDICATION

To Miguel Baja and all the other converts and fellow-workers whose stories I have told. Thank you so much for your partnership and the things you have taught me in terms of commitment and faithfulness to the task.

ACKNOWLEDGMENTS

The stories recorded in this book are a testimony of God's faithfulness and the powerful work of His Spirit. I accept responsibility for each mistake that was made and do not feel justified in taking credit for the fantastic results. If any human credit is due, it should be given to our entire family.

My wife, Elenor, was and remains a faithful, steady, uncomplaining partner in everything. We worked together as a team and our children contributed much, as they learned and understood the languages and culture of the people better than either Elenor or I did. They attended local Filipino schools and were effective in bringing the Good News to their classmates and school teachers.

The impact we had on our province and the surrounding areas was a family effort. I am exceedingly pleased that four of our children still serve in the Philippines—three of them as missionaries and one as a geophysicist working with another "missionary kid" on local infrastructure. I, therefore, dedicate this book to them and their children and pray for their continued faithfulness and effectiveness in serving the Filipino people and our beloved Master.

From left to right: Paul, Daniel and Steven (rear); Rebecca, Elenor, Richard and Debra

CONTENTS

OTHER BOOKS BY RICHARD VARBERG:

From the Iowa Farm to the Philippine Field:
40 Years of Church Planting in the Pearl of the Orient

To order, call (651) 917-1852,
or email rvarberg@chrcom.net.

INTRODUCTION

Less than a year ago I published my memoirs entitled From the Iowa Farm to the Philippine Field. It is a large book of 768 pages and tells the exciting story of my life and involvement in forty years of church planting in the Philippines. When I wrote that book, I doubted how well it would be received since it was my first attempt at writing a book. To my delight, it has received excellent reviews and the first edition is already out of print.

Several readers of my first book have encouraged me to do more writing. Some have commented that perhaps a shorter book would attract more readers. I, therefore, decided to write this book of short stories gleaned from my first book. I have rewritten each story in such a way that it can stand on its own and hopefully have a spiritual impact and application. I hope that the total impact of these stories will bring life changing decisions in the lives of the readers.

It is my prayer that many young people will be attracted to this book and find the stories interesting and challenging to the point they will seek further involvement in missions. I also hope many Sunday School teachers and church leaders will read these stories and retell them to increase interest and involvement in missions among their members.

My wife Elenor and I, with our three-month old son Paul, arrived in the Philippines in December 1958. We served with the Baptist General Conference Philippine Mission. After only a few days in Manila and Cebu City, we moved to Tuburan, Cebu. Tuburan was a small impoverished county seat on the west side of Cebu Island. The population of the county was about 48,000 people. About ninety-five percent of the people professed to be Roman Catholic.

When we arrived in Tuburan, there was a small group of Baptists that had been converted under the ministry of two previous missionaries. They were delighted to welcome us. The general populous also treated us cordially, but the leaders of the Catholic Church did their best to hinder our work. They wanted us out of town! I am sure that many of my readers will be very surprised by some of the stories they read in this book. Please keep in mind that the stories are not intended as a reflection of Catholics in general but are true and frank stories of what was occurring in our part of the Philippines in the mid twentieth century. That matters are continuing to change quite considerably around the world is another great story.

It should be remembered that Cebu is the Island on which Magellan planted the cross of Catholicism in 1521. Vatican II had not yet occurred when we arrived in Tuburan. The laity was taught that it was a mortal sin for them to read the Bible. To be a Protestant was worse than being a prostitute. A prostitute only sold her body; a Protestant sold his or her soul.

After spending four years in Tuburan, Cebu, and seeing the Tuburan church established, we moved to Masbate, where we served until 1997. There, too, we began with a small group of believers and saw the work expand not only throughout the island of Masbate, but also into several other islands including Ticao, Burias, and the southern part of Luzon. We saw the Masbate Baptist Church established, where I served as the senior pastor for some 30 years. This church planted scores of daughter churches, which have given birth to their own new congregations. We produced a daily radio program, "The Voice of Truth," that was aired very effectively for twenty years. We opened the Ikthus Youth Center, the Ikthus Dormitories, and Masbate Baptist Bible College. I served as the director of MBBC for many years and witnessed the training of many successful church planters and pastors.

Today there are Baptist churches in almost all of the twenty-two county seats in Masbate Province, and in scores of other county seats and villages throughout the region.

Elenor and I have five children, four of which were born in the Philippines. Two of our sons married missionary kids. Our oldest son, Paul, and his wife are serving as church planters in Tacloban, Leyte. Our second son, Daniel, and his wife together with our youngest daughter Debra and her husband are serving at Faith Academy, a school for missionary children near Manila.

Please read this book with an open mind and a prayer that God will show you how He wants you to become involved in the most exciting and meaningful adventure of all–sharing Christ with a needy world. If you are a true believer in Jesus Christ, ask yourself this question: Is there anything more important for me to do with my life than to share Christ with those who have never heard?

TIMELINE

1958	MAY: Richard Varberg graduates from Bethel Seminary.
1958	JUNE: Richard and Elenor are appointed as church planting missionaries to the Philippines by the Baptist General Conference.
1958	DECEMBER: Varbergs arrive in the Philippines and are assigned to Tuburan, Cebu.
1959	Miguel Baja, the father who posed the title question, asks Richard why he had not come sooner before his son died and went into eternity without knowing of salvation in Jesus Christ.
1960	OCTOBER 25: After a long battle, the Tuburan Baptist Church establishes the Tuburan Baptist Cemetery as the first Protestant cemetery in the province of Cebu.
1964	The Varbergs move from Cebu to Masbate, where they served for 33 years.
1964	The Masbate Baptist Church purchases the first of ten lots, which would become the location for its future ministry.
1965	FEBRUARY: The Masbate Baptist occupies its new church building.
1966	The Masbate Baptist Church opens the Ikthus Youth Center.
1966	Church planting begins with a "New Life Crusade" in Bantigue.
1968	The Masbate Baptist Church calls its first Filipino pastor.
1969	The first three gospel tracts are printed in the Masbatino dialect.

1969	Varberg designs and develops the first of three audiovisual vehicles to be used in evangelism and church planting.
1970	JANUARY 1: "The Voice of Truth" celebrates its inaugural broadcast, becoming a daily radio program that aired for 20 years.
1970	The Gospel of John is translated and published in the Masbatino dialect.
1972	The first of many poured concrete daughter church buildings goes up.
1973	The Masbate Pilot Project is proposed and adopted.
1973	A period of rapid growth and expansion begins involving many key centers and neighboring islands.
1979	SEPTEMBER 2: The Masbate Baptist Church commissions its first Filipino missionaries, Mr. and Mrs. Mardonio Marianito, to the island of Burias.
1981	The Masbate Baptist Church opens the Masbate Baptist Bible College with Varberg serving as its director until his retirement in 1997.
1982	JUNE 20: The Masbate Baptist Church dedicates its new "cathedral"; over 1,100 people attend.
1984	Mother Superior Sylvia Martinez finds the Lord.
1991	The Ikthus Dormitories are constructed and opened for occupancy.
1997	MARCH 17: The Provincial Board of Masbate passes a resolution "adopting Rev. Richard Varberg, Baptist Minister, as a son of Masbate Province, Philippines, and expressing grateful recognition for his missionary zeal in the spread of Christianity for more than thirty years."
1997	The Varbergs leave the Philippines with more than 100 churches planted. These churches are supporting their own Bible college and continuing to grow under 100 percent Filipino leadership.

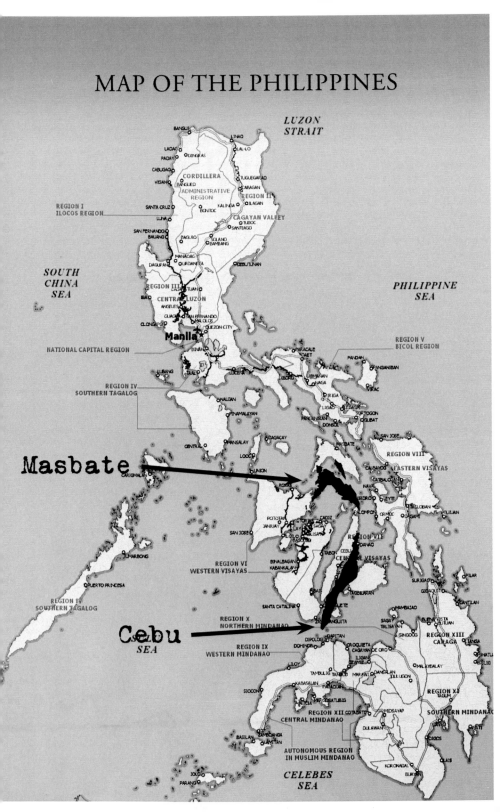

MAP OF THE PHILIPPINES

One

WHY DIDN'T YOU COME SOONER?

I t was hot! Very hot! Not an ideal time to be repairing the old 1953 Jeep station wagon. I always felt it important, however, to keep the Jeep in as good running condition as possible just in case there was another emergency.

There had been so many lately and I realized that this old Jeep had saved the lives of many critically ill or injured people living in the Tuburan area. Our Jeep was the only vehicle available for emergency cases. I was thankful that I had grown up on a farm in Iowa and had become quite skilled in repairing worn or broken farm machinery. This Jeep, however, was proving to be a real

Our maid with a beggar and our 1953 Willys Jeep station wagon

challenge. It seemed that everything that could break had broken several times. The missionary who had used the wagon before my arrival had already welded the differential back together more that once!

I was twenty six years old and my wife, Elenor was twenty four. We, with our infant son Paul, had now been living in Tuburan, Cebu for almost a year. The Baptist General Conference appointed us as church planting missionaries to the Philippines in June 1958. Our assignment was to follow two previous missionaries to the area of Tuburan. Tuburan was a county seat located on the west side of the Island of Cebu - the center of a population of some 48,000 people. It was a very underdeveloped area with no electricity or modern convenience of any kind. Though strongly Roman Catholic, it was noted for its witchcraft. Crime was widespread and there were many kinds of sicknesses. Tuberculosis was rampant. There were no local hospitals–the nearest were in Cebu City three hours away over rough, mountainous roads.

I was awakened many nights to rush critically ill or wounded patients to Cebu City. I remember one woman with twenty-six stab wounds. There was another whose neck had nearly been severed by a machete. We could actually see her spinal column. I held a lantern for over an hour while the local doctor tried to suture her neck back together as best she could before I rushed her over rough mountainous roads to a hospital. Why do emergencies almost always seem to happen at night?

As I continued working under the hood of the Jeep, I suddenly noticed movement out of the corner of my eye. I looked up to see an old man running down the street straight towards me. He stopped just short of my face and, puffing heavily, began begging for help.

"What do you want me to do?" I asked.

"He's sick, terribly sick!" he said. "You've got to help him!"

"Who is sick?"

"My son. He is terribly sick!"

"How is he sick?" I queried.

"He's very hot and he can't open his mouth!" he answered.

"Well, what do you want me to do?"

"Take him to the hospital," he begged. "If you don't help, my son is going to die."

"Where is your son?"

"In Bagasawi," he answered. "He's at our home."

Bagasawi is about three miles from Tuburan. Realizing that I was probably the only hope for his son, I decided to do what I could. I hurriedly put the Jeep back together and soon we were on the road.

When we reached Bagasawi, the old man, whose name I learned was Miguel Baja, led the way up a dirt trail to his house. As we entered the house, he pointed to his son, who turned out to be a thirty-year-old father of four, lying on a mat on the floor. I bent over him and placed my hand on his forehead. It was so hot that it seemed it would burn my hand. I have never touched a human body with such a high fever. I asked for a spoon and tried to insert it between his teeth to see if I could move his jaw. It wouldn't budge! Though I am not a doctor, I had enough experience to recognize that this was an advanced case of tetanus. Tetanus was still quite common in our area at that time—especially among infants whose umbilical cords were cut with a sharp piece of bamboo instead of a sterilized knife or scissors.

Because of the condition of the patient and the condition of my vehicle, we decided to take him first to the local government dispensary in Tuburan and seek the advice of the doctor. After examining the patient, the doctor advised against taking him over the long, rough road to Cebu City.

"Just leave him here," the doctor advised. "We will do the best we can for him."

We followed the doctor's advice but, as all feared, the man soon passed into eternity. The grief on the old man's face, as well as that of the wife of the dead man, made this an incredibly sad experience for me. I just couldn't get their faces out of my mind. I thought of the four fatherless children. I thought of the despair and hopelessness of life and death without Christ.

Since the members of the family were all Roman Catholics, I expressed my sympathies and then left them to perform their traditional ceremonies. This included taking the body to the local church and hiring the priest to "say a mass" for him and to sprinkle the casket with "holy water." Next would be the traditional nine nights of prayers for the dead (actually, nine nights of drinking and gambling), followed by a feast for all who came. This usually resulted in the family going into debt that might require months, sometimes even years, to pay.

A day or two after this feast, I was sitting at my desk, thinking about the Baja family. As I glanced at the shelf above my desk, I noticed that I had an extra copy of the New Testament in the Cebuano dialect, the language spoken by the Baja family. I decided to give this New Testament to them. I first wrote a few words on the flyleaf expressing my sympathies and stating that I was giving the book to them in memory of their son. I further explained that this book was the word of God, and that if they would read it and follow its teachings,

3

they would find the peace they were longing for. I then gift wrapped it and contacted one of the deacons to go with me to Bagasawi.

When we arrived, the Bajas were obviously still grieving over their great loss. I presented my gift to Mr. Baja and again expressed my sympathies. He took the gift and unwrapped it. He opened the book and read what I had written on the flyleaf. He thanked me for the book and for transporting his son to the doctor. He promised to begin reading the book.

About two weeks later, we returned and discovered that they had been reading and the Holy Spirit had already been working in their hearts. Before we left their home that day, Mr. and Mrs. Baja, as well as their widowed daughter-in-law, had accepted Jesus Christ as their own personal Savior.

Mr. Baja's conversion was especially remarkable. He was one of the leaders in his village. Though he was not wealthy by American standards, the village considered him well off as he was a landowner who had a house built of

Mr. Baja – typhoon

sawed lumber with a corrugated tin roof. He had been one of the village councilmen and was highly respected. Religiously speaking, he was a typical Roman Catholic who lived in sin and only went to church once or twice a year. He was considered a good Catholic, however, because he always gave a donation for the village fiesta and helped repair the chapel for this

yearly event. According to his own testimony, he often took part in drunken brawls and ran around with women.

When Mr. Baja accepted Jesus Christ as his personal Savior, he immediately stopped drinking and smoking, as well as several other vices. The whole family became regular attendees of the Tuburan church that I pastored. This meant they often had to walk the three miles to the church. Within a very short time, Mr. Baja, his wife, and daughter-in-law were baptized, and Mr. Baja was elected as one of the church deacons. A natural leader, he immediately began sharing his faith with his friends and neighbors. He studied his Bible and memorized many key verses. He had a great concern for the lost. He brought a new visitor with him to the church almost every Sunday.

"Why don't you spend more time in my village?" he asked me one Sunday after the service.

"Please remember," I replied, "I'm responsible for over forty villages. My time to spend in your village is very limited."

"Well, I believe that you ought to spend more time in my village," he replied. "I'll tell you what I am going to do. Every Thursday afternoon I'm going to take off from work. I want you to be there. We will visit my neighbors. We'll win them for the Lord!"

Needless to say, I was in Bagasawi almost every Thursday afternoon. Mr. Baja was always ready. We visited his neighbors and led many of them to the Lord. We began conducting regular Thursday afternoon Bible studies in his home. Soon, between thirty and forty regularly attended.

Mr. Baja also became concerned about his eldest son who had moved to the island of Mindanao some years before and knew nothing of their newly found faith. His burden became so great that he traveled all the way to Mindanao to find his son and bring him back to Bagasawi so that he could hear the word of God.

It was on one of those weekly visits to Bagasawi that an incident occurred that I will never forget as long as I live. When I arrived, Mr. Baja was waiting for me. "Come on," he said. "We're going up the mountain." Off he went up a trail. Needless to say, I followed.

We visited several homes up on the mountainside that afternoon. Mr. Baja first shared his testimony in each home and then, as best as I could, I explained the way of salvation. As the afternoon wore on and as we continued to climb farther up the mountain, I was huffing and puffing and wondering how long I could keep going at the pace he was setting. The humidity was so high, and it was so hot that I felt as though I would collapse at any moment. After what seemed forever, he looked back

Farmer plowing rice paddy

5

over his shoulder. Seeing my condition, he politely asked if I didn't think we should sit down and rest a while. I readily agreed and we sat down to rest in the shade of a tree.

After catching my breath, I took my Bible out of it's bag and began reading silently. I was sitting a little above the trail that went along the edge of the mountain. Mr. Baja was sitting just a little below the trail, some ten feet away. As I read, I realized that Mr. Baja was looking at me. I looked down at him and saw a very inquisitive look on his face.

"Yes?" I asked.

"Oh," he said, "I was just wondering how long there has been a missionary in this area."

I traced in my mind the history of missionary work in that area. Two missionary families had lived there before Elenor and I had arrived. Each had stayed less than three years. We had been there only a few months.

"I guess it is now more than five years," I replied.

"Five years! Do you mean to tell me that missionaries have already lived in Tuburan for five years?!" he exclaimed. I could see that he was shocked and that tears were forming in the corners of his eyes.

"Why do you ask?" I questioned.

"Well, do you remember my son?" he asked.

"You mean the one who died?"

"Yes," he answered. "The one that died."

"Oh, I certainly do." I replied.

"He was a good son. He was my favorite son," continued Mr. Baja. "I have been thinking about him all afternoon. He used to live up here on this mountain. These are his neighbors whom we have been visiting. As we have been sharing the gospel with them, I have been thinking about my son."

"What were you thinking?" I asked.

"I've been thinking about what a good son he was. I've been wishing that someone would have visited him and explained the gospel to him, just like we have been explaining it to his neighbors. If only someone would have, I am sure that my son would not have rejected. He would have accepted Jesus Christ as his Lord and Savior!"

6

Then with tears running down his face, Mr. Baja looked me straight in the eye and asked me the question I will never forget as long as I live.

"Sir, why didn't you come just a little sooner? If you would have, my son wouldn't be in hell today."

Then tears began running down my face!

This experience had a profound effect on my life. The fact that people were going to a lost eternity without having a chance to hear the wonderful message of life in Jesus Christ is a tragedy for which we, as a church, will certainly be held accountable. I feel certain that many of these lost souls would accept Jesus Christ if they were properly informed. Though I could not answer for the whole Christian church, I determined that day that I would reach as many as I could. This same determination drove Mr. Baja to become a very effective witness for Jesus Christ, and his contagious example inspired many others to do the same.

Two

TRUE COMMITMENT

When we took over the work in Tuburan there were about twenty five members of the Tuburan Baptist Church. The church building was a dilapidated thatched building on a street that many of the local people believed was haunted. As the work in Tuburan began to grow, the need for a new church building became evident. When a good lot for a church site became available, the church purchased it. When I informed the members that someone in the states had donated a hollow block-making machine to the mission that churches could now borrow, the members became excited.

"Let's build a hollow block church!" they exclaimed.

When I saw their enthusiasm to get started on a building, I gave a message on the secrets of a successful building program—using the building of Solomon's temple as an example. Pledges were made and preparations began. To further encourage the people, I built a plywood model of the proposed building and placed it in the front of the old chapel. Sand was hauled from a nearby riverbed and when the hollow block-making machine arrived, we began making blocks. Stones collected from nearby farms were mixed with the concrete for the floor and foundation. The proposed building would seat about 200 people. Each week, we set aside one or two days for volunteer work on the building. I worked right with the people. In fact, only one other member and I were strong enough to run the block machine.

It took many months but, gradually, the building began to take shape.

It was during this time that I noticed that Mrs. Baja did not seem to be her usual robust self. She had that look about her that I had come to recognize. One day I approached her and asked her how she felt.

"Fine," she answered.

I decided to probe deeper.

"Do you mean to tell me that you aren't coughing early in the mornings?"

"How did you know?" she asked in surprise.

"You're also running a fever every afternoon aren't you?"

"Well, yes, I guess I am."

"I think we should go to the doctor for a checkup."

With that, I called Mr. Baja and he agreed that we should take Mrs. Baja to the local doctor. After a careful examination, the doctor's diagnosis agreed with my suspicions—tuberculosis. The doctor prescribed three of the newly discovered "miracle" drugs to take daily for at least six months. She explained the danger of starting on this regimen and then stopping after a few weeks when the patient began to feel better. She warned that, then, the problem would get worse.

Tuburan Church

After we left the doctor's office, I also re-emphasized the danger of not completing the whole series. I explained how the germs would develop immunity to the drugs if they were not continued until the disease was completely knocked out. Both Mr. and Mrs. Baja promised that she would take the medicines faithfully every day until the completion of the six-month series.

Soon Mrs. Baja seemed to be her old self again. It was obvious that the medicine was doing its work. Then one day I thought I again noticed something in Mrs. Baja's appearance that caused me to suspect that she was not doing well. I asked her how she felt.

"Oh, just fine," she quickly replied.

By the color of her skin, I felt certain that she was not telling the truth. I went to Mr. Baja and asked him if his wife was taking her medicine. He just changed the subject.

"Hey," I insisted. "I asked you a question. Is your wife taking her medicine?"

Mr. Baja did not answer. He just looked down.

"Is she?" I again asked. This time my voice was more persistent.

Mr. Baja could not look me in the eye. He just looked down. When I persisted with my question, he finally answered.

"No, she is not."

"Well, why isn't she?" I demanded in an angry tone.

"Well, we talked it over as a family and we decided that it is more important that we give our money to the church than it is that she have medicine."

Then it was I who could not look him in the eye! I realized the depth of their commitment. I realized that they were more concerned with the success of the mission than I was. I realized that I could learn much from these babes in Christ.

To give a proper ending to this story, we did see to it that Mrs. Baja got her medicine, but it is this type of dedication that was to bring about the tremendous surge in growth that we were later to see in the churches of the Philippines.

Three

IT'S HOT IN THE PHILIPPINES

Few people living in the Western world realize the difficulty missionaries face in trying to adjust to the climate and culture of the land and people where they are endeavoring to work. Much of the success of any missionary, however, depends on how fully he or she is able to make these adjustments.

I am very grateful that Elenor and I were able to go to the Philippines when we were still young—I was twenty-six years old and Elenor was twenty-four. Usually young people can adjust more easily than older people. I am also grateful that I had four aunts and uncles, as well as several cousins, who served as cross-cultural missionaries. They often visited in my childhood home and shared their experiences with us. This gave me many insights as to how missionaries need to adjust to the many situations in which they find themselves. Growing up on a farm in Iowa with few luxuries made adjusting to a primitive situation much easier for me than for many. The required adjustments are never easy, however, and I suppose that none of us ever completely adjusts to a new culture and climate.

As far as climate goes, I had previously worked in Alaska and loved it. I told the Lord I was willing to serve any place in the whole wide world as long as it was cold. When God began to call us to the Philippines, I struggled with the prospect of living in a tropical climate. I never realized, however, just how oppressive tropical heat can be when you live at sea level just ten degrees north of the equator.

Leaving for Philippines -
1958 at Galilee

When we went to the Philippines in 1958, we spent less than a week in Cebu City and then quickly found ourselves living in the town of Tuburan, on the west side of Cebu island. There was no electricity, and the house that had been rented for us to live in had a tin roof and was poorly constructed for dissipating heat. During the day, the heat from the sun that radiated through the tin roof threatened to melt the skin right off from our bodies. The evenings were little better as the kerosene Coleman lanterns we used for lighting seemed much more efficient in producing heat than light.

At times, we would seek relief by turning off the lanterns and just going to bed, but even then we suffered because of the heat. Many were the nights that I awakened with the realization that my pillow was soaking wet from perspiration. Often, when I turned the pillow over to what I hoped was the dry side, I discovered that it was soaked clear through. How we longed for even one electric fan to keep the air moving!

Even Filipinos complained of the heat when they came to visit our house. They would soon excuse themselves and retreat to the shade of a coconut tree in the yard below. Before long, we decided to move to a different house near the seashore that had a roof made of palm leaves. We were thankful that palm leaves blocked much of the heat from the sun, and we also found that breezes blowing off the ocean felt much cooler than those blowing from other directions. Later, when I became the

Our first house
in Tuburan

property committee chairman for our mission, I did my best to find housing

14

for new missionaries that would be as cool as possible and have cross ventilation that took advantage of prevailing winds and, where possible, ocean breezes.

One result of the heat was that my legs became very itchy. Soon, they were bleeding as a result of my scratching. I couldn't imagine why they itched so severely. After several consultations with doctors, they advised that my body apparently could not adjust to the heat of the Philippines and that I should consider returning to the United

Home by the sea —
Tuburan house

States. I refused to consider that as a solution and eventually discovered that, in the heat of the tropics, I was allergic to many artificial fabrics and could only use clothing made of cotton, ramie, or some other natural fiber. Even then, I had to take three or four baths a day and scrub my legs exclusively with soaps such as Lux that contained no perfumes. If the itching became too severe, I found that scrubbing my legs with pHisoderm or pHisohex would usually bring relief. Both of these are special cleansing soaps used by doctors in the operating room.

The necessity of taking a bath three or four times a day can be a problem when there is a shortage of water. Beyond that, I found it necessary to change my trousers each time I took a bath, as my trousers very quickly developed salt streaks and looked like my overalls had when I worked on the farm in Iowa on hot summer days during harvest season. One four-year term, I took thirty-nine pair of trousers with me from the states and still ran out before the four years were up.

Four

LANGUAGE LEARNING IS IMPORTANT

Learning the language is one key to understanding a culture. Language learning is not easy. It involves much more than just learning a new vocabulary. One must develop new thought patterns and new sentence structures. Most Filipinos think and formulate their sentences in the passive voice, while we Americans usually think and speak in the active voice. I grew up saying: "Let me see that" when I wanted to see something. In dealing with Cebuanos, I had to learn to say: "*Kita-on ko ina.*" (It will be let by you to have it seen by me.)

I also discovered that their use of the passive voice reflects their great desire to say things in an inoffensive way. It seems they seldom say directly what they mean. They leave it up to the person to whom they are speaking to figure out what they mean. We Westerners often offend Filipinos by saying exactly what we mean. Doing this is especially offensive when one is dealing with interpersonal relationships and problem solving.

When Filipinos speak English, they often use the same word order that they use in their native dialects. This can be illustrated by what happened to me one day when we were having a meeting in the YMCA in Cebu City. They had just applied a new coat of paint to their swimming pool and its surroundings. To keep people from stepping on the wet paint, they put up a sign stating, "Keep off your feet!" I went to the person in charge to explain that their sign didn't say what they meant. He quickly informed me that it said exactly what they meant. I decided to say no more. I realized that I would not only have to learn how to speak their dialect but to also learn how to speak "Filipino English."

To be fluent in a language, one must not only learn new vocabulary and sentence structures, but also learn to pronounce words correctly. When I finally got to the point where I thought I was speaking Cebuano fluently, Filipinos still accused me of having an American accent. In trying to discover what I was doing wrong, I asked my informant to allow me to look into his mouth to observe how he formulated words. In the process, I discovered he did not allow air to come out of his mouth when articulating "t's" and "p's." I, however, was exploding them. If you are an American, I challenge you to hold your hand in front of your mouth and try to say "put" without allowing any air to escape from your mouth.

To learn how to articulate "t's" and "p's" without allowing air to escape from my mouth, I taped a small piece of paper to the tip of my nose so that the paper hung down in front of my mouth. I then practiced trying to speak sentences with many "p's" and "t's" without making the paper move. Eventually, I learned.

When we moved from Cebu to Masbate Island, I had to learn several different dialects. This brought language learning to a new level. I soon discovered that some words used in Cebuano were also used in other dialects. What was confusing is that sometimes these words have the same meanings—sometimes they do not.

One day, while teaching a Sunday School class on the book of Acts, I told about the apostle Paul going to Lystra and preaching the gospel. When I told of how he got stoned for it, a sergeant of the police force, who was attending the class, blurted out: "He got what he deserved!" I quickly realized that the word that I had used for preaching must have a different meaning in Masbatiño. I had used the word "sangyaw," which means, "to preach" in the Cebuano, Waray, and Ilongo dialects. I had assumed it also meant the same in Masbatiño. When I asked the sergeant what "sangyaw" meant in Masbatiño, he explained that it means to "raise cane" or "cause trouble." So if Paul went to Lystra and caused trouble and they stoned him for it, he got what he deserved.

Language learning is not easy for most people, but it is exceedingly important for a missionary working in a foreign culture. One will seldom understand a culture without knowing the language of that culture. Perhaps one of the best ways to show one's love for any people group is to learn their language.

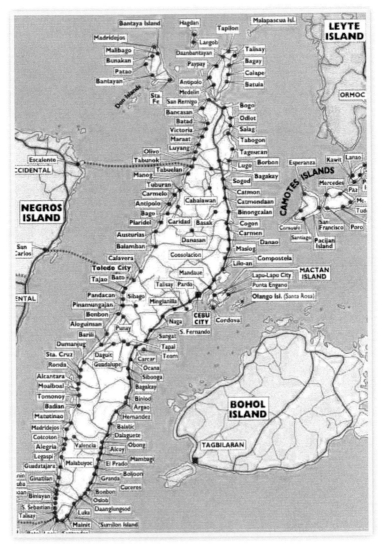

Cebu Province

Five

GOOD FOOD AND CLEAN WATER

Every culture and every country has delicious food. What one person considers delicious, however, may be considered distasteful by another. I grew up in a culture that loves cheese. Some of my favorites are Limburger cheese and bleu cheese. Just the smell of these cheeses can drive some people out of the house. When we were leaving for the Philippines, one older and experienced person gave me this advice: "When you go to the Philippines, take your sense of humor with you and leave your sense of smell behind." This was good advice. I also told the Lord, "Where He leads me I will follow and what they feed me I will swallow!"

When we arrived in Tuburan, Cebu, the Christians held a welcoming party for us. They had prepared a delicious Filipino meal for us. Someone had caught a large and very tasty fish. It had been roasted whole and placed in the center of the table. Since we were the guests, we were offered the most delicious part—the head. Both Elenor and I were stunned. Neither one of us had any idea of how to go about eating the head of a fish. It also bothered us having the fish eyes look up at us. After several events of being served this dish, we came to realize that the head of most fish is indeed the most delicious part. I usually avoid it, however, as it is quite fattening. Reared in the Philippines, our children loved to eat fish eyes and would sometimes quarrel as to whose turn it was to get them when a whole fish was served at our table. They were much more accepting at first than I.

The first time I smelled small, dried minnow-like fish (*ginamos*) frying in the kitchen, I thought something must have died. Some missionaries refuse to eat this very common food of Filipinos and will not even allow this fish to be cooked in their houses. It takes a long time for the smell to go away. Since returning to the states, I often long for a breakfast of dried fish and rice.

All in all, adjusting to the food in the Philippines was not difficult for us. We learned to love rice and the many tropical fruits such as papayas, mangos, pineapple, and bananas. At least once a day, we would have a delicious fruit salad. In Tuburan, vegetables were limited to green beans, Chinese peas, squash, eggplant, cabbage, and several spinach-type leaves. Since many of these leafy vegetables were contaminated with amoeba and other harmful organisms, we soon learned not to eat them raw. If we did decide to eat any raw fruit or vegetable that could not be peeled, we would first wash it in water mixed with bleach to try to kill all the germs.

Both beef and pork were available in the local market and we would order a chunk each week. When it was delivered to our house, we would wash off the dirt and brush away the flies and try to figure out what part of the cow or pig it was. Then we would either cut it appropriately or grind it into hamburger. We soon discovered that most steaks and roasts needed to be pressure cooked for a long time to make them chewable. Chickens could often be purchased from the numerous farmers walking by our gate. They were usually very good.

Good drinking water is a luxury in the Philippines. We found that the only safe drinking water was water that had been boiled for twenty minutes. This we did each day in our home. When traveling or visiting in the homes of others, we hesitated to drink the water. Sometimes, however, we felt we could not refuse and ended up drinking what was offered to us. When we did, we usually paid the dear price of getting amoebic dysentery. When visiting in the home of someone we felt we knew well enough that they would not be embarrassed, we would ask for a soft drink, which was usually available in the local *sari-sari stores*. It is amazing how Coke and Pepsi have been able to market their products worldwide! It is also amazing how good a warm bottle of Coke can taste when one is really thirsty. Fortunately, bottled soft drinks are usually sterile. Sometimes when visiting a farmer's home, I would ask someone to climb up a coconut tree and get a nut or two so we could drink the refreshing coconut juice. By the end of our missionary career, bottled water became available in most areas.

When traveling, we were usually forced to eat whatever was available in the local restaurants and hotels. A very amusing incident occurred when our fellow missionaries Fred Thomas, George Chalmers, Irv Bjelland and I were surveying Masbate Island. We had traveled to Masbate over night on the

Roasting a pig

Jacobo I, a rickety old launch that sailed between Hagnaya, Cebu and Placer, Masbate. I had been quite unsuccessful in getting much sleep, as my cot was right next to the huge mast. The engine had a huge flywheel and each time it fired, the mast squeaked loudly as it moved back and forth in the hole through the deck and down into the hull where it was placed.

When we finally reached Placer, we had to transfer from this launch to a smaller outrigger canoe to be shuttled ashore. After a breakfast of bread and coffee, we boarded a bus (a truck with wooden benches) bound for Cataingan, where we hoped to negotiate renting a house for our fellow missionaries, the Harvey Esplands, who were planning to move there. The roads were terrible and the rental negotiations lengthy. Late in the afternoon, we were able to leave Cataingan and proceed on to Masbate City, the capital of the province. It was past sundown when we arrived, and since the town had no public electricity, the streets were dark and dingy.

As we neared the center of the town, we saw a lone electric bulb illuminating the sign of the Sunshine Hotel. It looked old and very rundown, but we were starving. My companions headed straight for the hotel while I took care of some other business. When I had finished, I climbed the rickety stairs to the second floor of the hotel and entered the dining room.

"Come on, Dick," Fred called. "We've got steak for supper! We've even got ice in our Cokes!" We had been drinking warm Cokes all day long. When

23

the waiter came for my order, I first asked if there was a place where I could wash my hands.

"Sure," he answered. "Come with me to the kitchen."

When we arrived in the kitchen, he pointed to a pipe coming through the wall with a faucet on the end. I bent over the pipe, and after turning on the faucet, began washing my hands. As I washed, I noticed a huge pile of dirty plates beside me on a table. Several cats were busy washing them! I jumped when I heard a crack behind me. I turned to see the waiter return an ice pick to the table and then go to pick up the chip of ice that had scooted across the floor when he had chipped it off a block of ice lying there. The waiter placed the chip of ice in a glass and came over to fill the glass with water.

Later, when the waiter came for my order, I asked that my steak be "well done." I also specified that I wanted my Coke in the bottle.

"They can't put ice in the bottle!" Fred interrupted, with a queer look on his face.

"I've been drinking Coke warm so long that I have learned to like it that way," I answered. "By the way, since you guys have already eaten, why don't you go out to the kitchen and clean up?"

Fred immediately got up and went to the kitchen. Soon, he came back and looking at me rather angrily, exclaimed, "Why didn't you tell me?!"

"Sorry, it was already too late," I responded with a grin.

In spite of taking all of the above-mentioned precautions, I often came down with amoebic dysentery after we moved to Masbate Island. Masbate was noted for its amoebic problems. One of the sources of the problem was that there were many open sewers with public water pipes passing through them. Some of these pipes were old and leaking. Then, when the water was turned off in a certain section of town, the sewer water would seep into the pipes. Many of the patients in the local hospitals suffered from amoebic complications. My wife, Elenor, once got amoebic hepatitis. The situation was terrible. At one time the water became very smelly at our church and eventually stopped completely. When we called the water officials to investigate the problem, they dug up the four inch pipe in front of our church and found it was plugged up with a dead snake. During the later years of our stay in Masbate, I usually took a series of amoeba killing drugs four to six times a year. Some people thought the discomfort caused by taking the drugs was worse than that caused by the amoeba.

My uncle Arthur Nyhus, who served as a missionary in China during the 1930s, told me about the problems they faced with amoebic dysentery. The only remedy available to them was to drink kerosene. This was very dangerous. If they drank too much it would kill them. If they coughed while drinking, the kerosene would get into their lungs and create real havoc.

I sometimes wonder how many times the apostle Paul got sick eating the food and drinking the water available to him on his missionary journeys. I can only imagine what he must have had to eat and drink while he languished in prison dungeons. His testimony, however, was: "I know what it is to be in need, and I know what it is to have plenty. I have learned the secret of being content in any and every situation, whether well fed or hungry, whether living in plenty or in want. I can do everything through him who gives me strength."

Six

BUGS

Ants of many kinds are very common in the Philippines. The large red ants can inflict a very painful bite and should be avoided. Most people living in the Philippines have, at one time or another, stepped on a red ant's nest and found ants crawling up their legs and into their clothes—biting as they go. It can be amusing to watch people stripping off their clothes trying to get free from these pests.

The smaller ordinary ants, however, do not have such a painful bite and Filipinos pay little attention to them. They are often found crawling on the food that is served. These ants love sweets and the sugar bowl is their favorite dining room. I have heard people comment: "You can tell whether a person is a first, second, or third term missionary by his or her reaction to finding an ant floating in the coffee. A first-term missionary will refuse to drink the coffee; a second-termer will just take a spoon and remove the ant and proceed to drink the coffee; a third-termer can be found looking for ants to put in the coffee!"

Cockroaches are found in almost every building in the Philippines and reproduce prolifically. Most hotel rooms have at least a few of these pests. Everyone living in the Philippines has a continual battle to keep them out of their house. Fortunately, there are now various chemicals that are quite effective in killing them, but the battle persists. I have awakened more than once to find a cockroach drinking the fluid around my eyes!

There is also a very small biting gnat that is very common in the Philippines. They are attracted to light and are small enough to go through window screens if a light is turned on in the house at night. I am quite allergic to the bites of these gnats and they troubled me greatly when we lived in a house near a fishpond. Fishponds seem to attract gnats. I minimized this problem, however, by installing lights under the eaves of our house on the outside of the screens. The gnats and other bugs would then congregate around the light outside of the screens, instead of inside. Fortunately, the small lizards that crawled around the walls and ceilings of our house considered both gnats and mosquitoes a delicacy, and if any got through our screens, they eagerly assisted us in eliminating them.

Centipedes and scorpions are also quite common in the Philippines. Elenor and I were shocked one day to find a two-inch long centipede in the crib right next to our son, Dan, when he was only about two months old. We were told that if it had bitten Daniel, it could have killed him.

When we first arrived in Tuburan, Cebu, I often went visiting our contacts' homes with a deacon as my companion. I usually enjoyed these visits and learned much about Philippine culture while making them. One thing puzzled me, however. I could not understand why my arms and legs would swell up and itch for days afterwards. One day, as Mr. Gonzales and I were walking home from a visit, I shared my problem with him. To my amazement, he began to laugh.

"What are you laughing about?" I asked.

"Don't you know what that is?"

"No I don't," I answered, "What are you talking about?"

"Didn't you notice that the chair you were sitting on was crawling with bedbugs?"

"Bedbugs!" I exclaimed. "What are bedbugs?"

I remembered my mother saying, "Good night, sleep tight, and don't let the bedbugs bite," but I had never actually seen a bedbug and had no idea what they looked like. To my dismay, I discovered that almost all houses in Tuburan at that time were infested with bedbugs! I am allergic to bedbug bites and this proved to be a real problem for me. It wasn't until months later that I discovered a secret that would help me deal with this problem. The subject came up as we were making plans to invite a visiting Filipino evangelist for some evangelistic meetings. The question was: "Where can he stay? Who will house him?"

Mrs. Esmero, an older Christian woman who had just transferred to Tuburan from Negros Island, volunteered that she would be happy to house him if we would help her with her bedbug problem.

"Do you have bedbugs?" I asked.

"Yes, plenty of them!"

Since she was a licensed government mid-wife, I asked her how she handled the problem for herself.

"Oh," she said, "we just put old newspapers on the floor before we roll out our banigs (sleeping mats). The bugs can't smell through the paper."

There was my solution! From that time on, when I went visiting, I would plan a strategy to outsmart the bedbugs. I would first look around the room to see if there were any old newspapers or magazines lying around. If I spotted one, I would walk over and pick it up. Then, while pretending to read it, I would look for a place to sit down. I would then place the newspaper or magazine on the spot where I intended to sit. If there were no magazine or newspapers to be seen, I would simply sit on the bag in which I carried my Bible. Usually, by the time the bedbugs discovered that I was on the other side I was ready to leave anyway!

One day, while visiting a supporting church in up-state New York during our first furlough, I was asked to speak at a Saturday morning men's breakfast. It was in the fall, and that Friday night we had the first hard frost of the year. When I arrived at the church, the men were complaining about how cold it was. I, however, was rejoicing that it was a hard frost. When the men asked what was so great about a hard frost, I asked them the following question: "Did you ever stop to think how many bugs died last night?" After I told some of the above stories, they got my point.

Seven

DRESS APPROPRIATELY

During our first term in the Philippines, I came to appreciate Mrs. Esmero very much. She was an older, mature Christian who had transferred from Negros Island to Tuburan on the Island of Cebu where we were living. She was about fifty years old and had some association with American missionaries in Negros. She loved the Lord and was not afraid to give advice to a young man in his late twenties trying to become a successful missionary. One day, after the worship service, she asked if she could speak with me privately. I immediately agreed. When we found a private place, she asked me if I had a pair of white trousers. I confirmed that I did.

"Do you also have a Barong (the Philippine fancy dress shirt)?"

"Yes," I replied, "I have one."

"Then please wear them when you preach," she advised. "We Filipinos have grown up seeing the priests wear clerical robes when they preach. We expect you to also dress in a garb appropriate to your position in our church."

Up until that time, I had just worn an ordinary pair of trousers

Wedding picture shows formal dress in Philippines

and a short-sleeved sport shirt. From that time on, I was careful to dress appropriately for each occasion. I found it to be very important in gaining the respect of the educated people. Even the poor people appreciated it. I found that at that time it also meant that I should not wear short pants in public, no matter how hot it was. I envied the missionaries serving in India, where the English colonizers had established the custom of wearing short pants even on formal occasions.

In the Philippines, even poor people are very conscious of how they dress in public. Many mountain people will walk barefoot down the mountain and then stop to put on their shoes when they reach the town. They don't want to wear out their shoes just walking to town.

Most Filipinos dress very casually in their own homes. When a visitor arrives, however, they will not show themselves until they have dressed appropriately.

One day, the "grapevine" brought a rather puzzling report about the Chalmers—missionaries who lived in Catmon on the east side of the Cebu Island. At that time, they were our closest American neighbors, as the crow flies. The Filipinos reported, "The Chalmers allowed their children to run around naked!"

This report rather disturbed me, and I decided to make a quiet investigation to see if it was true. I discovered that the Chalmers were allowing their smallest children to run around clothed with nothing but a panty or diaper because of the severe heat. They were "naked" in the eyes of a Filipino. The Filipinos, however, allowed their children to run around dressed in only a t-shirt. They were considered fully dressed. When I questioned Filipinos about this practice, they answered: "A person never gets pneumonia in his bottom. He gets it in his chest."

As I thought about their reasoning, I somewhat agreed with their logic. I also agreed that the Filipino practice made a lot of sense for people who could afford neither diapers nor a washing machine. When a child's bottom is bare, all that needs to be done when an accident occurs is to dip the dirty bottom in the ocean or hold it under a faucet for a few moments and the problem is solved.

Eight

BICYCLES BETTER THAN CARS?

Tuburan, Cebu was known for its strong opposition to any religion other than the Roman Catholic religion. I was told that the first person to own a Bible in Tuburan was hung by his neck in a well until he told where he hid is Bible so it could be burned. The priests taught that it was a mortal sin for a layman to read the Bible. I was also told that the first person to attempt to preach the gospel in Tuburan was a young evangelist named Aliño. His preaching, however, almost cost him his life. When he began preaching, the people threw stones at him and, without a doubt, would have killed him had he not run to a house, locked the front door behind him, and then run out the back door into the darkness. He got away and decided then and there to quit the ministry and become a lawyer. He determined that he would defend Protestants in their attempts to spread the gospel. Aliño became my legal advisor when I was later harassed.

The Catholic Church strongly opposed our ministry as well. I was called a "white devil" and harassed in various ways. I also discovered the Catholic Church put great pressure on the people not to allow us to visit in their homes.

R.C. Cathedral in Tuburan

One of the problems was that many of the people we visited were tenants and did not own the land on which their houses were built. Often, landlords threat-

Typical farmer's house

ened that any tenant who allowed us to visit on their property and preach this "false" religion would be forced to move out. Even though the Philippine constitution guarantees religious freedom, tenant farmers were sometimes forced off the farms they had tilled for many years because of their Protestant faith. I, therefore, decided that when I went on visitation, it was best for me to be as inconspicuous as a blond, 200-pound American could be. Our 1953 Willys Station Wagon parked in front of a house gave away my presence immediately, so I decided to order a good bicycle from the states to use for visitation purposes. I felt that it would be easy to hide a bicycle while I was visiting in a home.

When the bicycle arrived, however, I used it very rarely. I discovered that after riding just a few blocks, I was perspiring so profusely that my clothes were ringing wet. I did not feel I was fit to visit in homes looking like a drowned rat.

Later on, Dr. Jack Hill, an American Missionary doctor who was the director of Chong Hua Hospital in Cebu City, solved my problem when he offered to sell me his Vespa motor scooter. "It starts immediately but won't stay running," he said. "I'll give it to you for a very cheap price. Maybe you can fix it."

I looked it over and decided to buy it. I soon discovered that the tail pipe was plugged with carbon. I rammed a screwdriver into it, twisted it a few times, and the engine ran perfectly.

Sometimes it is good to be as visible and conspicuous as possible; sometimes it is better if you are not seen at all! Jesus encourages us to be "wise as serpents and harmless as doves." (Matt. 10:16 KJV)

Nine

RURAL PHILIPPINE HOUSES

When we arrived in the Philippines, most rural houses were made of native materials. They were usually built on posts with the floor from one to five feet above the ground. If the people were poor, much of the building, including the posts, was made of bamboo. If the people could afford it, the upper-structure and the posts were made of either sawed lumber or round wooden branches of trees. Often, the walls were of either split bamboo or thatch. The roofs were usually made of Nipa leaves woven together.

These houses are very cool and practical. The farm animals are often kept under the house at night for safe keeping from thieves. Chicken nests are hung in corners of the kitchen. When staying in these homes, my hosts sometimes asked if I would like an egg for breakfast. If I said, "Yes," all the cook had to do was reach up and grab a fresh egg from one of the nests and crack it into the frying pan.

The way large families could squeeze into a very small house amazed me. Shortly after we arrived in Tuburan, Cebu, the wife of Lois Briones, one of our new members, gave birth to twin daughters. The family was very poor and lived on a farm near the village of Suba. Their home was a small hut about ten feet square , with a small lean-to that served as a kitchen. The stove was nothing

Plowing with water buffalo

but a tin pail with a hole cut in the side through which they fed sticks to the fire that had been lit in the bottom. A caste aluminum pot or frying pan was placed on top of the pail in which each meal was cooked. One small chest, the size of a toy box, contained all of the clothes and personal effects of the whole family. This was the only piece of furniture in the house. A woven mat, rolled up in the corner during the day, served as their bed at night. In this house lived a family with six children—including the newly-born twins. The eldest child was five years old.

When Mrs. Esmero, the midwife from our church, was called to deliver the twins, she had to tear up the mother's only dress to make temporary blankets for the twins. She estimated that each child weighed about two and a half pounds at birth. When we were informed of the situation, we brought some food for the family and some receiving blankets and shirts for the babies. Amazingly, the whole family appeared to be very healthy. I had to make a cultural adjustment when Mrs. Briones brought the twins to church and nursed both of them at the same time while sitting in the front row about four feet from the pulpit!

When the church in the neighboring town of Tabuelan began to grow, we gained many new contacts. Some of these were from a village north of town. One day, Joel Villamor, a student from the Baptist Bible School of Cebu, and I decided to visit in that area. We had one contact that lived on a farm. When we arrived at his house, we were invited in. I climbed up the ladder and then stepped from the lean-to kitchen into the living room. When I stepped into the living room, there was a loud cracking sound and the whole house collapsed just as I jumped back out the door!

Upon investigation, we discovered that the main beam supporting the house had been eaten hollow by termites. It was obvious the owner of the house was just as embarrassed as I was, so after expressing our regrets, Joel and I went on our way. I was too embarrassed to ever go back to that house! I did learn from that experience, however, to be more careful before taking my 200 pounds into an obviously dilapidated house. It is much better to converse under the shade of a nearby tree.

Jesus instructed his disciples to shake the dust off their feet if a home or town would not receive them. He never mentioned what to do if our entering a house caused it to collapse!

Ten

PRIORITIES

As I became more fluent in the language and as our presence became more widely known, many opportunities opened for outreach to the neighboring villages. I, however, was kept very busy in the areas where we already had begun work. It bothered me tremendously when I had to turn down any request to come to a new area. There just wasn't enough time and energy.

As I tried to evaluate my situation, I found that I was spending a tremendous amount of time, energy, and money trying to meet the physical needs of people. Some weeks, I would make as many as three emergency trips to Cebu City—rushing gravely ill or injured patients to the hospital. Often, I would miss almost a whole night of sleep. I would sometimes try to catch a nap during the day, but this was almost impossible because of the tremendous humidity and heat of the tropics. We had no electricity so I didn't even have the benefit of an electric fan. I never did learn how to fan myself while sleeping. Even at night, I often awoke because of the heat.

One night, as I lay in bed trying to fall asleep, I pondered my situation. One of the biggest challenges was to set proper priorities. The many demands for my time and energy forced me to say "No" to many good things. Good is so often the enemy of best! This particular night, I was questioning the amount of time I spent on the medical emergencies that consumed so much of my time. It seemed that they were interfering with my reaching out into new areas with the gospel. But, how could I say "No" to someone in dire physical need?

As I pondered this question, I experienced something I will never forget. It was as though I heard a voice speaking to me: "Dick, don't you realize that I can heal every sick person in this whole area simply at the snap of my fingers? That is completely in my control. There is, however, something that I cannot do. I cannot save these people against their will. I have given them a free will. I sent you here to preach the gospel and with it to enlighten their minds and influence their wills so that I can save and heal them. Preach the word as I commanded you to, and see what I will do."

This seemed to me a direct revelation from God, but all through my ministry, I have continually struggled to find the proper balance between helping people with their physical and their spiritual needs. Many people say that you can't talk to a man about his soul if his stomach is empty. This is not true. Often I have found people in dire physical need to be very receptive to the gospel. I also discovered that I can help save a person's physical life, but if that person does not get right with God, he or she will soon be back in just as bad a situation as before I lent a helping hand. On the other hand, I have found that if a person gets right with God, his or her physical problems are greatly minimized. So many of their physical problems are the result of sins in their lives.

As requests continued to come from unreached areas for us to come and preach the gospel, I often felt very frustrated. I realized that in each area people were dying every day without any hope. But, I also realized that if I said "yes" to one area, I was saying "no" to the others—at least for the time being. I came to realize the tremendous responsibility that had been given to us as Christ's disciples. I realized what Jesus meant when he said to Peter, "I will give you the keys of the kingdom of heaven; whatever you bind on earth will be bound in heaven, and whatever you loose on earth will be loosed in heaven" (Matt. 16:19). Peter used the gospel message to open the door to the kingdom of heaven for the Jews in Acts 2 and 3,000 souls came under the reign and rule of Christ; he opened it for the Samaritans in Acts 8 and for the Gentiles in Acts 10. The key that he used was the gospel message. Now I had that key, and I realized that though the death of Christ was sufficient for all, it was only efficient for those who had the privilege of hearing the message. When I made a decision to use the keys and open the door to one area as opposed to another, it seemed I was acting as God, deciding who could or could not go to heaven.

I felt a tremendous load on my shoulders and mourned the fact that there are so few missionaries. Why aren't there enough to go around? Somehow, I knew that it wasn't God's fault—Christ died for the sins of the whole world—He commanded us to go to Jerusalem, Judea, Samaria, and the whole world. He is not willing that any perish. I found myself echoing the word of the apostle Paul: "How, then, can they call on the one they have not believed in? And how can they believe in the one of whom they have not heard? And how can they hear without someone preaching to them? And how can they preach unless they are sent?" (Rom. 10:14-15)

Eleven

PUBLIC DEBATES

One night, a rather prominent person in town invited me to come to his house and share the gospel. Shortly after I arrived, we were rudely interrupted when a heavyset man burst into the house demanding to know what I was doing there. I responded that I had been invited by the owner of the house to help him study the Bible. The interrupter, whom I later discovered to be Mr. Macoy, the principal of one of the schools in town, retorted that this could not be allowed. When I asked him why, he stated that I was teaching false doctrines. When I asked what false doctrines I was teaching, he tried to illustrate. As a young apologist, I was ready for him and proceeded to defend my beliefs from the Bible and to refute his. It turned out to be a real debate that lasted until 10:30 that night. At that time, Mr. Macoy stated that, though he had to leave, the battle was not over. He would gather his men and we would meet again.

As I evaluated what had happened, I realized that God had aided me in knowing what arguments and what verses to use. I had, however, been merciless and, perhaps, rather rude in response to the attacks of Mr. Macoy. Because of Mr. Macoy's shouting, several people had gathered to see what was going on. I obviously won the debate and had completely humiliated my opponent in front of the owner of the house, as well as the people who had gathered. I had won the debate, but because I humiliated Mr. Macoy publicly, I also gained an enemy.

Later, when I realized what I had done, I determined that if I were again forced into a debate, I would seek to debate in such a way that I would gain the respect and friendship of the person with whom I was debating, as well as that of the audience. Humiliating someone publicly and causing him or her to lose face is not generally a good strategy for missionary work! It is much better to graciously, but strongly, defend the truth and seek to win the respect and friendship of the person attacking you. In future confrontations, I was able to learn better how to do this.

When Joel Villamor, a brilliant student from the Bible School, agreed to come and assist in the work in the town of Tabuelan, we decided to have an open air meeting every Wednesday night on the street near the chapel. We were able to gather a crowd of up to 200 people by showing filmstrips and then after a crowd had gathered, we would give a gospel message.. Many people were showing interest in what we had to say. .

This greatly provoked the Catholic Church. In an attempt to counteract our progress, they immediately assigned two "Catholic Defenders" to harass us. These men actually carried identification cards to prove that they were official "Defenders." They had been trained by an Italian priest named Jose Bosch. He felt it was his mission to organize and train Catholic laymen to defend the Catholic Church. He was himself a very rude and uncouth man. While we were conducting an ordination service for Pastor Batuto in Cebu City, he had disturbed and interrupted the service. He used an amplifier to shout out insults and then even sang "cowboy songs" right outside the chapel—dedicating them to Pastor Batuto. He also stood at the door of schoolrooms where missionaries were conducting release-time Bible classes and offered five centavos to each student who would agree not to attend. The two defenders that were assigned to harass me were brothers. Their family name was Ruelan.

Each Wednesday afternoon, when Joel and I arrived to do visitation, they were ready for us. They followed us around and challenged us to debate. One day, I decided to take them up on their challenge as many people were gathering. Though I now understood the Cebuano language quite well and taught and preached in it regularly, I decided that I would use Joel as an interpreter during the debate. This would help me ensure that I was understanding any hidden meanings in what they were saying, and it would also give me time to think of what I was going to say next while Joel was interpreting what I had just said.

The first debate went very well, and my opponent went down in defeat. This could not be tolerated, so he immediately challenged me to debate him again the following week. To this, I agreed. I did my best to be friendly to him and to not humiliate him publicly. I had learned the fallacy of humiliating an opponent in my previous debate with Mr. Macoy.

Soon, I found myself in a public debate with the Catholic Defenders in Tabuelan almost every week. There was very little entertainment of any kind in that town, so people came to get in on the excitement of a debate. These debates turned out to be very different from anything I had experienced in the states. I discovered that one could win a debate logically and Biblically, but, if you didn't get the crowd on your side, you would lose. The Iglesia Ni Kristo, a local Philippine sect, which was also challenged to a debate by the same "Defenders," also realized this. To ensure that they had the crowd on their side, they brought four truckloads of their members as their cheering section when they debated.

One day when we arrived in Tabuelan, we were informed that, on that particular day, the debate would be handled differently.

"You will be facing two debaters today," they informed me.

"Two against one will not make a fair debate," I objected.

"So you are afraid," concluded my opponent in a smart-alecky fashion.

"No, I am not afraid," I answered, "but two against one doesn't seem right."

When it was obvious that the crowd was on their side, I finally agreed to take on both of their debaters at the same time. They then proceeded to inform me that the procedure of debate would also be different on that day.

"We will ask questions," they stated, "and you must answer either 'Yes' or 'No.'"

"Wait a minute," I objected. "There are some questions that cannot be answered 'Yes' or 'No.'"

"Any question can be answered 'Yes' or 'No,'" they replied.

The crowd was laughing, and it was obvious that I would lose unless I could somehow get them on my side. Suddenly, I got an idea.

"All right," I said, "I agree to answer any question that you ask 'Yes' or 'No' provided that you first answer one question from me with a 'Yes' or 'No' answer."

When they hesitated, the crowd began to shift to my side, and they realized that the tables had turned. They could not refuse if they wanted to win.

"All right," they asked, "what is your question?"

"How many children do you have?" I asked, "Yes, or No."

The crowd roared their approval, and I won the debate!

In these debates, I continually endeavored to befriend my opponents. The debates were held in front of the Pamflona Store, and the owner would usually give us a snack afterwards. As we ate our snacks, I had many friendly discussions with my opponents. Soon, one of them began coming to our house in Tuburan, where I had the privilege of sharing the gospel with him privately. Sometimes I would suggest that we just read the Scriptures together without either one of us making any comment.

One day, after we had read through the book of Galatians, Mr. Ruelan commented: "That book must have been written by a Protestant."

I thought for a while that he was actually going to surrender and accept Jesus Christ as his own personal Savior. To my knowledge, however, he never did. At least he came to know and understand the truth.

Few of us can understand the pressure he was under, and how difficult it was for him to break with the Catholic Church. How we need to pray for our Roman Catholic friends! Many of them are now reading the Bible, but all of them find it very difficult to break with the Catholic Church.

Twelve

TWO ATTEMPTS ON MY LIFE

One night, I was rudely awakened when Elenor jabbed her elbow into my ribs.

"What are you doing?" I asked, with no little irritation in my voice.

"Look!" she gasped, pointing out the window.

We were sleeping in an upstairs bedroom with the windows wide open. There was a tree just a short distance from our window from which one could step or jump to a canopy-type awning that extended about three feet out over the first floor window below. On this branch was a man just getting ready to step onto that awning and enter our bedroom! I jumped up immediately and ran out the door hoping to catch him, but he got away.

Since I wasn't able to catch him, I came back into the house and was soon sound asleep again. When I think of it now, I marvel that I could go back to sleep so quickly. The only thing that I can say is: "When you serve the Lord, He gives the courage needed to face whatever difficulties or dangers that come your way."

The next day, I reported the incident to the Chief of Police. He assured me that he would put our house under surveillance. Sometime later, I saw the Chief and asked him if he had been able to catch anyone.

"Yes," he answered, "we caught him."

"Did he confess?" I asked.

"Yes, he confessed," was his reply.

"Did it take any pressure?"

"Yes, it took some pressure."

I knew what that meant. In that town the method of pressuring a confession from a suspect was to grab him by the neck and force his head down towards a pail filled with human dung and repeatedly ask: "Did you do it? Did you do it?" In similar circumstances, I'm afraid I would confess whether I was guilty or not!

The Christians would sometimes advise me not to be out alone at night.

"If you aren't careful, they'll get you!" was their warning.

I am not easily frightened and was often out after dark. One dark night, I was walking alone down a trail near our home. Several hundred feet down the trail, I could see a lamp burning in the window of a little hut. The typical lamp in those days was nothing but a small tin can filled with kerosene and a wick installed in a hole punched in the lid. When lit, these lamps made about as much light as a large wooden match makes when struck.

As I focused on this lamp, I saw something flash in front of me. My reflex action caused me to grab at it and I caught an arm coming down holding a thirty-inch bolo (machete). I immediately raised my knee with as much force as I could muster and caught the owner of the arm in such a way that he went flying up into the air. I retrieved him on the way down, and since I was much bigger and stronger than he, I soon had the machete and was carrying him back down the trail towards our house.

When we neared our house, there was enough light for me to recognize my assailant. He was the son of a schoolteacher who lived near our house. I called to the father, and when he appeared on the balcony of his house, I threw the son up onto the balcony. I then invited the father to come down and retrieve his machete. I later found out that this son had been trying to court one of our maids. She had refused him because he wasn't a Christian. He apparently attributed her refusal to my influence and decided to take out his wrath on me. The family was so embarrassed by this incident that the boy later decided to leave town.

Thirteen

A PIG PROBLEM

One night while we were living in Tuburan, Cebu, I was awakened by someone shouting: "Sir, Sir, Tabang intaun!" (Sir, Sir, Please help!)

"Oh no, not again!" I said to myself as I wearily crawled out of bed.

I looked out the window. I could faintly see several people standing just outside our gate.

"What do you want?" I called from my window.

"Sir, please help. She'll die if we don't get her to the hospital as soon as possible." I wearily dressed and went down to the gate.

"What's happened?" I asked. In the darkness, I recognized a local midwife, Mrs. Esmero, in the group.

"This lady lives way up in the mountains," she explained. "She's been stabbed many times and lost a lot of blood. If we don't get her to the hospital within two hours she'll be dead!"

"There is no way we can get her to the hospital in two hours!" I exclaimed. "It takes at least three hours to get to Cebu City."

"We must try to save her!" pleaded Mrs. Esmero. "I'll go with you and we'll do everything we can to keep her alive."

Mrs. Esmero was a member of the church—a wonderful Christian midwife—and I could not refuse her pleadings. Together we had made many harrowing trips to Cebu City endeavoring to save lives. How could I refuse, if she, much older and perhaps much more tired than I, was willing to go? I hurriedly prepared the old 1953 Willys Station Wagon for the trip. I removed the back seat and placed a rubber air mattress on the floor. We then lifted the groaning patient onto the mattress. As I observed the condition of the woman, it seemed almost useless to even try to transport her over those roads! She was obviously in a very critical condition.

"Come on! We've got to hurry!" cried Mrs. Esmero.

I started the Jeep and we took off. It was 2:00 in the morning. I drove as fast as I dared. One thing that often encouraged me to drive fast on emergency runs was the smell! Unless you have experienced it, you cannot imagine the odor coming from a person who has been injured after working in the fields all day and is covered with blood, dirt and perspiration. This lady had obviously been oozing blood for several hours. She lived several hours' walk up in the mountains. They carried her down on an improvised stretcher. I discovered that if I drove with the front windows open, the odor decreased with the increase in speed. Now I had two reasons to drive fast!

As we bounced along, the road was completed deserted. No one appeared to be moving at that hour of the night. Soon, we were approaching the town of Tabuelan. I knew that I should slow down upon entering the town but decided to push on at full speed. The patient's life might be snuffed out at any moment! The town was absolutely dark, as there were no streetlights. It appeared that everyone was asleep.

Then it happened! I must have been going at least thirty miles an hour—top speed for those roads! I saw it simply as a moving shadow coming from the right side of the road. There was a thump and I felt the Jeep bounce. I instantly knew what it was. I had run over someone's pig!

A pig is of great value in the rural Philippines. Each family tries to have at least one pig at all times. The pig serves as the family bank. Any extra food is fed to the pig. The pig is the insurance policy. If someone gets sick, dies, or if there is an emergency of any kind, the pig is sold to cover or, at least, help cover the expenses. Perhaps the expression "piggy bank" originated from this practice.

"What should I do?" I wondered. If I stopped, I knew the woman would die. If I didn't, our ministry in Tabuelan could be in jeopardy. What would people think if they discovered that I had run over someone's pig and hadn't even stopped? As I peered ahead into the darkness, I saw someone coming down the road. I quickly stopped and told him what had happened. I asked him to please notify the owner of the pig that I would be back in the morning. We then sped on.

We made it to the hospital in slightly over two hours and thirty minutes. The woman was still breathing as we carried her into the emergency room. I breathed a prayer of thanks to God. I looked down at the woman, and for the first time could see her face clearly. She opened her eyes, and looking intently up at me, she whispered a very faint "Salamat" (Thank you).

The emergency personnel at the hospital took over and I wearily went back to my jeep. It was starting to get light, so I decided to go to the Baptist Guesthouse for a cup of coffee and something to eat. Marv and Ruth Lindstedt were at that time managing the guesthouse and became accustomed to my coming in at almost any hour of the day or night and were always gracious in supplying my needs. I was glad that this time I wouldn't have to awaken them, as I observed the maids were already up preparing breakfast. It was great to have people running the guesthouse who understood my situation and were always ready to share not only food and a place to rest, but also sympathy, comfort, encouragement, and guidance when it was needed.

When the Lindstedts awakened, we enjoyed a hearty breakfast together. I told them of my experiences of the previous night. They encouraged me to get some sleep before striking out again. I thanked them but explained that I needed to get on my way. Not only did I have a busy schedule planned for the day, I now had a "pig problem" to deal with!

It was almost noon by the time I arrived at Tabuelan.

"I've got so much work to do today," I said to myself, "I'm going to solve this 'pig problem' the American way. I don't have time to do it the time consuming Filipino way ."

When I reached the part of town where the incident had occurred, I stopped the vehicle to inquire where the owner of the pig lived. The first person I asked appeared to know all about the incident and immediately pointed to the owner's house. It was obvious that the dead pig had already become the "headline" of the morning gossip column.

I went to the owner's house and, standing at the foot of the stairs leading to the second floor, I called out *"Maayo, maayo."* In the Philippines, it is typical to call out a greeting rather than to knock on the door.

Soon, an elderly gentleman appeared at the head of the stairs. I politely greeted him and explained that I was the one who had run over his pig. As he came down the steps, I apologized for what had happened and explained that I had been forced to drive fast in an effort to save a wounded person's life. I told him that the patient was now recovering in the hospital in Cebu City, and that I had come to help pay for his pig that had been killed. I then reached into my pocket and pulled out a five-peso bill. Handing it to him, I said, "I hope that this will cover my share of the damages."

"Five pesos!" he shouted. "I paid twenty pesos for that pig! That pig was worth twenty pesos!"

When I saw how angry he was, I realized that this problem could not be solved in the American way. No matter how tired I was, no matter how much of a hurry I was in, I would have to take the time to do it the Filipino way.

I stepped back from the steps and looked around. Seeing a log that was obviously used as a bench, I walked over and sat down. After some time, the man walked over to the same log and sat down only a short distance from me. I waited silently and then when I thought it was appropriate, I introduced myself and asked him for his name. He did not answer immediately, but eventually he looked up and gave me his name. I asked how old he was. Age is respected in the Philippines, and he answered quite proudly that he was sixty years old. I looked at him, showing amazement and said: "If you are that old, I'll bet you can remember when this road was built, can't you?"

"Oh yes," he answered, "I remember it well."

"How come they built this road?" I asked

"They built it when the automobiles came in," he answered. "They built it for the automobiles."

"Do they have any rules or regulations regarding the use of the road?" I asked.

"Oh yes, they've got lots of rules regarding the road," he answered.

"Can you give me any examples?" I asked.

50

Amongst other things, he mentioned that farm animals are not allowed to run loose on the road.

"Then how did it happen that your pig was loose on the road?" I asked.

"I guess I forgot to tie him up last night," he answered rather sheepishly. I could see that he was aware of where I was going with my questions.

"Now, you and I have a problem," I proceeded.

"Yes," he said. "It's a twenty peso problem! You killed my pig! I paid twenty pesos for that pig!"

"What happened to the pig?" I asked.

"You killed it!"

"No. I mean, what happened to the pig after I killed it?"

"Well it was dead, so we ate it," he said.

"Was it good?"

"Oh, it was delicious!" he exclaimed. "We fed that pig well!"

"How much would it cost to buy that much good pork at the market?" I asked.

"You couldn't buy that much good meat for less than ten pesos," he proudly exclaimed.

"Now," I said, "you and I have a problem."

"Yes," he interrupted, "it's a twenty peso problem!"

"But who got the meat?" I asked.

"We did," he answered slowly.

"Then wouldn't it be proper to subtract the value of the meat from the twenty pesos?" I reasoned.

"Yes—I guess that would be right," he responded hesitantly.

"Now then," I reasoned, "we had a twenty peso problem and we've gotten it down to ten pesos. Both of us have admitted to doing something wrong. I was driving too fast in an effort to save a person's life, and you forgot to tie up your pig. What would you think if we just split the difference? You pay five. I pay five."

He suddenly looked up with a rather amazed look on his face and exclaimed, "Why, that's an excellent idea!" He then proceeded to call his neighbors. He explained to them our agreement, and told them what a wonderful guy I was.

He then pocketed the same five-peso bill that he had so vehemently refused some forty minutes earlier. We were now friends instead of enemies.

It takes longer, but it pays to do things their way!

> *"Though I am free and belong to no man, I make myself a slave to every one, to win as many as possible. To the Jews I became like a Jew, to win the Jews. To those under the law I became like one under the law (though I myself am not under the law), so as to win those under the law. To those not having the law I became like one not having the law (though I am not free from God's law but am under Christ's law), so as to win those not having the law. To the weak I became weak, to win the weak. I have become all things to all man so that by all possible means I might save some. I do all this for the sake of the gospel, that I may share in its blessings." (I Cor. 9:19-23)*

Fourteen

A TERRIBLE ACCIDENT

I will never forget another incident that occurred in 1960. The Lindstedts had moved to Bogo and were teaching in the Bible School. I had another emergency run to Cebu City. When I arrived at the Southern Islands Hospital in the middle of the night, I was surprised to see Marv Lindstedt, coming out of the hospital. He was white as a sheet!

"What's wrong?" I asked.

"I had a terrible accident!" he answered. "I went out to pick up our mail. As I passed by the high school, the noon bell rang and the students came running out the door. One student ran into the street heading for the park across the street where he planned to eat his lunch. He was looking backward as he called for his friend to follow. I saw him coming and slammed on my brakes. I was able to stop my vehicle, but since he wasn't watching where he was going, he ran right into the front of my car. He hit his head on the hood ornament and fell over unconscious. I picked him up and took him to a local doctor there in Bogo. After examining him, the doctor told me that he thought he would be all right. He added, however, that if I wanted to be sure, I should take him to Cebu City. I wanted to be sure so I brought him here to Southern Islands Hospital. He just died!"

One of the first instructions other missionaries gave us when we arrived in the Philippines was this: "If you ever have an accident while driving a vehicle, if your vehicle can still be driven, keep going. Go to the nearest police station and ask to be locked up in the jail." The reason for this advice is that Filipinos often lose control when an accident occurs. This is especially true if the one injured is a relative. They often take the law into their own hands.

Marv had not followed these instructions. He had overlooked his own personal safety in his attempt to help the victim. I knew, however, that he was in danger now that the boy had died.

"You'd better get out of here," I advised. "I'll take care of things."

I immediately went to the patient's hospital room. The body was still there with the father and grandfather in attendance. I introduced myself as a friend of Mr. Lindstedt. The family name of the victim was Ngnho.

"I have come to help you." I explained. "Have you paid for the hospital bill?"

When they answered in the negative, I told them that I would pay it for them. I then went to the business office to pay the bill and get the cadaver released from the hospital. When I returned to the room, I asked the father if he would like to have his son embalmed.

"Yes," they answered. We, therefore, loaded the body into my Willys Station Wagon and drove to a funeral parlor.

"Would you like to have your son dressed in a new suit?" I asked Mr. Ngnho, the father. He seemed very pleased with the idea, so I took him and the grandfather to a department store and purchased the suit of their choice. I am quite sure that this was the first suit the boy, or any member of his family, had ever worn.

"Is there anything else that I can do for you?" I asked.

"Yes, there is," they answered. "Take us home."

They explained that they lived on a farm near Bogo and that they had no way to transport the body home. I knew that it would be difficult to get anyone to transport a cadaver to Bogo unless we hired the hearse from the funeral parlor. This would be very expensive and to get anyone else would be almost impossible. Many Filipinos believe that if a dead body is transported in a vehicle, that vehicle will soon fall apart. The nuts will come off the bolts and the screws will come out. I also knew that it would be very dangerous for me, a friend of Mr. Lindstedt, to go near the house of the deceased. No one could predict what would happen. They might take out their frustrations on me.

As I considered the matter, I decided to take the risk. I felt that I should do everything possible to convince the family that both Lindstedt and his friends were good people. I called Marv at the guesthouse to inform him that I was taking the body to Bogo. I asked him to contact the insurance company and tell them what had happened and ask that an adjuster be sent to Bogo. The authorities kept Marv in Cebu City.

The long trip to Bogo was uneventful. As we neared the farm home of the family, I began to wonder if I was doing the right thing. I had no idea how the family would react when I arrived on their turf. I prayed for guidance and protection.

When we arrived at the trail leading to their house, I stopped the car. When the family recognized who we were, people began to appear from all directions. My situation didn't look good! As we unloaded the body, I informed them that I would return the following morning to discuss a settlement with them.

"We'll be waiting for you," they answered. I was very relieved that they seemed to show no animosity towards me. As they began carrying the body up the trail, I drove off. I spent a restless night in Lindstedt's home wondering what the next day would bring forth. Ruth Lindstedt feared their missionary days in that area were over.

The next morning, the insurance adjuster arrived. We discussed the situation and decided that it would be wise to request Attorney Lepiten to go with us. His father owned the private school the boy had been attending. He was also a friend of the mission. Fortunately, he was willing to go.

When we arrived at the trail leading to the farmhouse, I parked the Jeep at the edge of the road. As soon as the relatives saw us coming, they put up a terrific wail. Somehow, I felt that the wailing was mostly for our benefit.

As we walked slowly up the trail and neared the house, they motioned for us to come in. We did our best to express our condolences and show our concern and friendship.

After some time, I asked if there was any quiet place where we could go to discuss what had happened. They nodded and one of them led us further up the trail to the top of the mountain. There, on the top of the mountain, was a huge old house built on stilts. They motioned for us to climb up the stairs leading to the living quarters.

As I reached the top of the stairs, I entered what might be called a foyer. As I passed through this room, I noticed a large numbers of long machete knives stacked in one corner. I shuddered as I realized why they might have been placed there.

I proceeded from the foyer into an unusually large room for a farmhouse. At one end, a short bench had been placed facing a semi-circle of benches. I figured that the short bench belonged to my companions and me. I sat down in the middle of the bench. The attorney and the insurance adjuster sat on either side of me. We waited for some time before anyone else entered the room.

The first to enter was a very large, old man. He seated himself at the very center of the semi-circle of benches. Then entered another old man, but younger than the first. He seated himself to the right of the first. Following him was another old man who seated himself to the left of the man in the center. This procedure continued until the benches were filled. I soon realized that the oldest man in the center was the great grandfather of the deceased. On either side of him were the two grandfathers. The uncles were next. The father of the dead boy was on the end to my left.

I waited for some time for something to happen. No one spoke. They all just stared at me. I soon realized that they were waiting for me to make the first move.

With a prayer for wisdom, I stood up to speak. I spoke in their native tongue—the Cebuano dialect. I told the story of a wonderful loving family—the Lindstedt family. I told of how the Lindstedt family had grown up in a faraway country. I explained how they had decided to leave their beautiful country and travel far, far across a very wide ocean to help the people of Manchuria, a part of Northern China. I told how they had helped so many people find peace and happiness.

I then told of how they had given birth to several children. One of them was named Marvin. He was a very good son, and after he had reached maturity, he left his parents and went to the states where he could receive a good education. While he was studying, he learned about the many needy people of the Philippines. He decided that he would give his life to help the Filipino people.

I told of how he and his family had now lived in the Philippines for several years. They had spent their time helping people. I told of how everything seemed to be going fine until yesterday, when a very terrible accident occurred.

"You all know what that was," I said. I explained how very sad Mr. Lindstedt was about what had happened.

"Now," I said, "I have come here as Mr. Lindstedt's friend and representative to see if something can be worked out so that we can all be friends and not enemies."

I then sat down and waited for their response. They all just sat there staring at me. It seemed an eternity before the old, white-haired man in the middle began clearing his throat. He then slowly and deliberately gave one of the most eloquent speeches I have ever heard in the Cebuano dialect. He told the story of a simple mountain family. He told of how poor they were as humble farmers. He told of their love for each other—how they all worked together towards common goals. He told of a dream they had. It was a dream that someday they would be able to break out of their poverty. They had planned together. Their plan was that, someday, by pooling their resources, they would be able to send one of their descendants to school. They would choose the one that showed the greatest potential. He would become somebody! Through him, their family would be liberated from their poverty. He then proceeded to tell of how they had chosen one of his great grandsons.

"Everything was going fine until yesterday," he said, "when your friend killed him! Now," he continued, looking me squarely in the eye, "you say that you have come to negotiate a settlement. I hope that you have a good plan, because if you don't, we do!" He then sat down.

As I thought of what that plan might be, I could not help but remember the stack of machete knives I had seen in the foyer. I prayed again for wisdom as I stood to speak.

"If there were any way that we could bring your son back to life again, we would do it," I began. "But, you know and I know that that cannot be done. The best that we can do is to somehow try to help you and comfort you in your sorrow. As you know, we have already paid all of the expenses incurred at the hospital. We have paid for the embalming of your son and bought him a new suit. We purchased a beautiful casket for him. We brought him home in our Jeep. And," I continued, "We will also buy a big pig for your funeral feast."

At this point I proceeded to explain the laws of the Philippines. "If Mr. Lindstedt were proven to be at fault in the accident," I explained, "it would be his responsibility to pay 3,000 pesos to your family." I made it clear, however, that I was not there to admit fault on behalf of Mr. Lindstedt.

"Let's not get into an argument about who was at fault," I advised. "If I were to ask you, I am sure that you would maintain that Mr. Lindstedt was at fault. On the other hand, I am also certain that Mr. Lindstedt would maintain that your son was the one at fault because he ran into the vehicle after it had stopped. You will remember that your son was not run over, nor was he thrown a distance away by the impact. He simply collapsed in front of Mr. Lindstedt's vehicle after he ran into it and hit his head on the hood ornament. The best thing for us to do is to talk about a settlement and not to try to establish liability."

As I looked at them I knew they were wondering what I was leading up to. I gave them time to think over what I had stated. I knew they had most probably spent much of the previous night discussing what kind of an offer I might make.

"Besides what we have already expended, I am prepared to pay you 1,500 pesos for your loss," I continued in all sincerity.

"One thousand five hundred pesos!" the old man interrupted. "You must pay us 3,000 pesos!"

"No," I reasoned, "I cannot pay 3,000 pesos because paying the full amount would be an admission of fault. I cannot admit fault on behalf of Mr. Lindstedt. Only the courts can establish fault, and I certainly hope that this case does not need to go to court. We want to be your friends—not your enemies. We want to make an amicable settlement with you."

The old man continued trying to convince me that we must pay the full 3,000 pesos. I, however, refused to budge. I maintained that paying the full amount would be admitting guilt and I could not do that.

At last, the old man realized that he was making no progress and turned the negotiating over to the boy's grandfather to his right. I recognized him to be the grandfather on the mother's side of the family.

"If you cannot pay more than 1,500 pesos, then could you give us a Christmas present?" he asked.

"More payment I cannot give," I reiterated, "but when you, the bereaved, ask us who have come here to comfort you for a Christmas present, it is very difficult for us to refuse." In the Philippines, one can ask for a Christmas present any time of the year, under certain circumstances.

"Just what type of Christmas present would you like?" I asked.

"My son-in-law is in grief," he explained, referring to the father of the deceased. "I don't want him to grieve. I want him to take a vacation. I want him to go to the city. If he wants women, I want him to be able to afford women. If he wants to go to the movies, I want him to be able to go to the movies."

"I cannot understand your suggestion!" I interrupted. "For your son-in-law to be running around with women would only increase the grief of your daughter. She is the mother! She is also in grief! I can have no part in anything that would increase her pain. But," I continued, "I do agree to the plan of having your son-in-law go on a vacation."

"What kind of expense do you estimate would be involved in such a vacation?" I asked.

"Oh, I think that 500 pesos would be sufficient," he answered.

At this point I recounted the expenses that we had already incurred amounting to almost 1,500 pesos. I then reiterated that we would also supply a big pig for their funeral feast.

"In addition to all of this," I continued, "we will *give* you the 500 pesos Christmas present you have requested, but we will only *pay* you 1,500 pesos."

I reiterated that they must understand that only the 1,500 pesos was being given as a payment. The rest was a gift from us to them as an expression of our sympathy for their loss.

"This is, of course, contingent upon your willingness that we remain friends and upon your willingness to sign the legal documents that our attorney has prepared releasing Mr. Lindstedt from any further liability in this case," I clarified.

At this point, and only at this point, did the old man in the middle turn to the father of the victim for his approval. When the father nodded his head, the case was closed. The papers were signed in the presence of the attorney and we all shook hands.

It was with thankful hearts that we walked back through the foyer containing the machete knives and down the trail to our waiting vehicle.

"You ought to be an insurance adjuster," exclaimed the insurance adjuster. This was the first time he had spoken during the whole affair. I, however, had no aspirations of changing occupations. For me, there is no greater calling than being God's representative, bringing good news to a foreign land. How wonderful to serve one who could solve such impossible problems as the one we had just faced!

What rejoicing there was in the Lindstedt household when we broke the news of the settlement to them! By the grace of God, they were now able to continue serving in that area for many more fruitful years.

Later the Lindstedts did have some suspenseful days. The local police chief became very angry when Marv refused to pay him a $1,000 bribe for not charging him with the crime of "homicide through reckless imprudence." A trial followed with its dangers. Throughout the trial, the Ngnho family refused to take revenge against Marv, and one family member even witnessed on his behalf. The charges were eventually dropped just two weeks before the Lindstedts were due for furlough in the spring of 1963. Years later, we have learned that some of the Ngnho family have now been converted.

As I evaluated what had taken place, I was amazed to note that the forty-year-old father had been given no part in the direct negotiations described above. He was only asked to give his consent to what his elders had negotiated. Does this not tell us something about who we should approach first when seeking to evangelize a new area?

> *"Now to him who is able to do immeasurably more than all we ask or imagine, according to his power that is at work within us, to him be glory in the church and in Christ Jesus throughout all generations, for ever and ever!" (Eph. 3:20-21)*

Fifteen

THE FIRST PROTESTANT CEMETERY

PART ONE

Many people in Tuburan were becoming interested in the gospel but hesitated to take a stand for Christ because of pressure from the Catholic Church. One of these people was Ezekial Albaño . The local priest had become very vocal in his attacks on both our teachings and on us personally.

"If you become a Protestant, they will have to throw you in the ocean when you die. We won't allow you to be buried in our cemetery, and, as you know, there is no other," he announced publicly. A member of the Jehovah's Witnesses died, and when the priest would not allow him to be buried in the cemetery, his relatives left the cadaver in the Municipal Building until the government finally buried it because of the odor.

Some priests were teaching that it was better to become a prostitute than a Protestant. "If you become a prostitute you are only selling your body; if you become a Protestant you are selling your soul," was their rationale.

In the Philippines, great emphasis is placed on having a proper burial. Many times I would hear relatives refusing to spend money to buy medicine for a member of their family. "There is only enough money for the burial," was their reasoning.

Mr. Albaño was under deep conviction. He wanted to accept Jesus Christ. He hesitated, however, because we had no Baptist cemetery and the Catholic Church had been able to block the establishment of a municipal cemetery.

"What will happen if one of my children dies?" was his question. I continually assured the people that, if any of our members died, we would make sure that there would be a decent burial.

Finally, Mr. Albaño could resist the Spirit's promptings no longer. He called for me to come to his house. When I arrived, he was ready to accept Jesus Christ as his Lord and Savior. Two weeks later, one of his daughters died.

"Now, what shall we do?" I asked myself.

When I discussed the situation with the deacons, they suggested that we go to the owner of the land on which a former Catholic cemetery was located. They told me that they sometimes had allowed people to be buried there—especially if relatives of the deceased had previously been buried there. When we arrived at the home of the landowner, we found him to be very friendly and sympathetic. He was a relative of one of our deacons.

"I have no objection," he stated, "provided you get a permit from the Regional Health Department. Just send them a telegram requesting a permit and then go ahead and bury. So far they have always agreed and issued a permit."

Mr. Albaño agreed to the plan and we proceeded with a funeral service in the chapel. We then marched in procession carrying the coffin to the cemetery. Many people saw the procession and followed to see how Protestants would bury their dead.

At the gravesite, we sang several songs and then I gave a message on the subject of death. I explained that for a Christian, death was actually the door to heaven. I explained that when a person accepts Jesus Christ as his own personal Savior he is completely forgiven and cleansed from his sin. Cleansed completely from sin, his soul then goes directly to heaven when he dies. I also explained that the whole concept of purgatory was not in the Bible. People listened very intently, and it turned out to be a wonderful opportunity to share the gospel.

This was my first funeral service in the Philippines. Everything had gone very well, but in my heart I was concerned—knowing that burying in a closed cemetery was not a long-term solution to the problem. I knew that if I were not present, it would be difficult for the ordinary members to get a permit to bury in the closed cemetery. Somehow we must get either a municipal cemetery or our own private cemetery before I could feel free to leave Tuburan.

Not long after the burial of the Albaño daughter, Hammer Ceballos, a member of the church, came to our house early one morning to inform me that his wife had given birth to a stillborn child. After expressing my sympathies, I asked him what he wanted to do.

"Let's bury her in the closed cemetery like we did with the daughter of Mr. Albaño," he suggested.

"Okay," I answered, "I'll send a telegram to the Regional Health Department for a permit."

As Hammer was walking slowly away, I pondered why God had allowed another death in our midst. During the six years since the work had been begun in Tuburan, these were the first deaths in our Christian families. As I continued to ponder the situation, a thought suddenly came to my mind. I ran after Hammer and called him back to my office.

"Hammer," I asked, "Why do you suppose God allowed your daughter to be born dead?"

"I don't know," he answered with a puzzled look on his face.

"Do you suppose that God allowed this to happen to give us an opportunity to use your daughter's burial as a test case?" I asked. "The argument of the Health Department in refusing to give us a permit for our own cemetery has always been that there is already a cemetery in Tuburan. When we have pointed out that it is a Catholic cemetery and the priest will not allow us to bury, the Health Department has always maintained that we can bury in the

Catholic cemetery. They have maintained that when the Catholic Church requested a permit for their cemetery, they signed a document stating that they would provide a place for non-members. We even have a letter from the Health Department stating this in writing but the priest and local officials will not respect it. The town council even diverted the funds that had been appropriated by former President Magsaysay for a municipal cemetery in Tuburan to another purpose. We need a test case to bring this whole issue to a head."

I continued to explain to Hammer that it would be difficult to use the death of an adult member or even an older child as a test case because we would have already known that person as living person. There would be many memories. The person would already have become an integral part of our family.

"In your case, Hammer," I continued, "You have never known your daughter as a person. She was born dead. You have never known her personality. You have no memories of her actions. Would you be willing that we use her in a test case by attempting to bury her in the Catholic cemetery?"

Hammer thought a while and then nodded his approval.

"Let's do it!" he said. "This could be God's plan for my child!"

I went with Hammer to the home of the Municipal Secretary, Berting Mercado, the person in charge of issuing burial permits. When he saw us, he greeted us and asked what he could do for us.

"We have a cadaver to bury," I answered. "What shall we do?"

"You have a cadaver to bury, then bury it," he said.

"Where?" I asked.

"In the cemetery."

"What cemetery?" I asked.

"There is only one cemetery in this town—you bury it in the cemetery," was his emphatic answer.

"Yes," I said, "but it's a Catholic cemetery."

"You can bury in the Catholic cemetery. Just make sure that you dig where the porter tells you to bury."

"What kind of a permit do we need?"

"Only the government permit, which I will issue," he responded as he reached for a burial permit form.

"Can we hold a service in the cemetery?"

"Yes, you can hold a service there."

"The priest isn't going to like this!" I said.

"So what, he can't stop you!"

"I think that it would be best if you go with us to the cemetery," I suggested.

"When are you planning to bury?" he asked.

"At three o'clock this afternoon."

"Okay," he said, "Go to the cemetery this morning and dig the grave in the spot where the porter instructs you. Show him this permit. Then at three o'clock I will go with you."

When the men from the church got to the cemetery and showed the porter their permit, he instructed them to dig the grave outside the gate in the place reserved for unbaptized Catholics and for suicide cases.

That afternoon at three o'clock, we all gathered at the church and began waiting for the Municipal Secretary. After a rather long wait, someone suggested that perhaps he was embarrassed to walk in a Protestant funeral procession and would be waiting for us at the cemetery. We decided to proceed to the cemetery.

When we got there, the Municipal Secretary was nowhere to be found. When we proceeded to go towards the gravesite, the porter met us carrying a long machete and demanded to know where we were going. I told him we were going to bury a cadaver in the grave that the men had dug.

"Where is your permit?" he asked.

We showed him our official government permit.

"This isn't signed by the priest," he retorted. "No one buries in this cemetery without the signature of the priest!"

I pointed out that there was no place for the priest to sign. It was a government permit.

"You don't bury in this cemetery without the signature of the priest on the permit!" he shouted defiantly.

By this time, the mission had worked for almost four years trying to get a cemetery. Even Attorney Aliño had given up because of the opposition and power of the Catholic Church in Tuburan. I decided that now was the time for us to make our stand. I shoved the machete carrying porter aside and proceeded to the gravesite. The Christians followed me and we began our service.

We had just begun when I heard someone yelling. It was Mr. Esmero, the right-hand man of the priest. He had run barefoot the whole mile from the Convent, the priest's residence, to the cemetery to stop us.

"Get out of here! You can't hold a service in our cemetery!" He then continued shouting all kinds of insults at us.

I turned to him and said, "Listen, Mr. Esmero, we are here following instructions from the government. We have a permit from the government. Don't disturb our service. If you don't believe that we are here legally, file a case against us. We'll settle this in court."

"Okay, I will!" he shouted.

"If you'll wait just a few minutes, I'll give you a ride to the Municipal Building," I offered.

"I wouldn't ride with you for anything!" he shouted, and took off for the Convent.

We then continued our service but just as we were finishing, the priest arrived. We took off but left one man behind to see what would happen.

Later, we were informed that after we left, the priest ordered the body to be exhumed. When someone went to get a shovel, the ex-mayor, Mr. Alcantara, arrived. He was the landlord of most of our members in Suba and a secret sympathizer of ours.

"Father," he said, "you touch that cadaver and you'll go to prison."

The priest thought a minute and realized that perhaps the ex-mayor was right.

"All right, I'll make those Protestants dig it up!" retorted the angry priest. With that, he took off in a huff for the Municipal Building.

I decided that we should go to the Municipal Secretary's home. I wanted to know why Mr. Mercado had not kept his promise to accompany us. When we got there he asked how the burial had gone. When we told him, he said, "Fine, you did exactly what I told you to do. Everything is fine."

"No, it isn't," I countered. "Someone could have been killed out there! Both our men and the porter were almost ready to fight it out!"

"Yea, but they didn't. Everything is okay," he said with a smile.

"That may be what you think, but I am not sure the mayor will agree with you. Let's go and see the Mayor," I suggested.

"Okay, let's go," said the Municipal Secretary.

When we got to the mayor's house, we told him what had happened. He smiled and said, "You did just what you were instructed to do. Everything is fine."

"No, it isn't!" I insisted. "Someone could have been killed out there. Now you, as the mayor of this town, are responsible according to the law to see to it that there is a Municipal Cemetery established in this town. You haven't done it. Either you give us a cemetery or you give us your word of honor that the next time we have someone to bury you will give us a police escort."

"Okay," the Mayor answered, "I give you my word of honor. You will have a police escort next time."

Sixteen

THE FIRST PROTESTANT CEMETERY

PART TWO

When we left the Mayor's house, I decided that we could just as well make things a little hotter.

"Now, who has the best situation?" I asked our members as we walked back to the chapel. "We or the members of the Catholic Church?"

"What do you mean?" they asked.

"Well, if a Roman Catholic has a body to bury, how much does it cost?" I asked.

"Usually between forty and fifty pesos," they answered.

"How much did we pay?" I asked.

"Only fifty centavos for the government permit," they answered.

"See, isn't our situation better than that of the Roman Catholics?" I asked. They caught on immediately and began grinning from ear to ear. I suggested that they spread the news around town.

As I expected, things really got hot. It became obvious that the priest was going to file a case against us. The Municipal Secretary, fearing what would happen, suggested that I send the following telegram that he had prepared to the President of the Philippines.

Complaint—Pres. Garcia   October 25, 1960
PCAPE MANILA

ROMAN CATHOLIC PRIEST TUBURAN CEBU OBJECTED
BURIAL SECOND TIME DECEASED PROTESTANT IN CATHOLIC
CEMETERY STOP NO OTHER RECOGNIZED CEMETERY
EXISTS IN TOWN STOP KINDLY INTERVENE FOR US STOP
SUCCEEDED INTERMENT BUT RELATIVES HARASSED BY
CATHOLICS AND LIVES ENDANGERED PLEASE RENDER
OPINION THIS MATTER INSPITE RULING BY BUREAU OF
HEALTH CTC SEPT TWELFTH NINETEEN FIFTY FIVE QUOTE
ALL EXISTING CEMETERIES IN THE TOWN CANNOT REJECT
THE BURIAL OF ANY CADAVER IF THE PERMISSION OF THE
ADMINISTRATOR IS SOUGHT UNQUOTE.

REV RICHARD NEAL VARBERG
BAPTIST MISSIONARY
BAPTIST PASTOR

Though I would not have thought of sending such a telegram myself, I decided to follow the advice of the Municipal Secretary, Mr. Mercado. He pointed out that there was no charge to send a telegram of complaint to the President.

We got an immediate response from the Chief Justice stating that an investigation would be made by the Regional Health Department. I, therefore, decided to go to the Regional Health Department office in Cebu City. The priest also took off for Cebu City to file a case against us in the Court of First Instance.

When I arrived at the Regional Health Department and introduced myself as Rev. Varberg, the person at the receiving desk jumped up immediately and politely asked me to sit down. It was obvious that I was expected.

Soon, a group of three or four doctors entered the room and asked what they could do for me.

"Well, if you will sit down, I'll tell you a story," I suggested.

They sat down and I gave them a history of our attempts to get a Municipal Cemetery established in Tuburan. I then told of the most recent incident and of our attempt to obey the previous instructions of their office to bury in the Catholic Cemetery.

"We'll go to Tuburan right now and see to it that you get a Municipal Cemetery or even a private cemetery—whatever you want," was their immediate response.

This was the very office that had previously refused to help when Attorney Aliño was hired by the previous missionaries in Tuburan to help get approval for a cemetery. Apparently, they had received a rather harsh rebuke from the Chief Justice.

"Okay," I said, "I have been asked to appear before the Town Council on Monday morning at 9:00. Why don't you appear with me?"

"Yes, we'll be glad to do that," was their immediate response.

"You can stay at our house while in Tuburan," I offered. "My wife will be glad to prepare food for all of you."

"Oh, we couldn't do that," they replied. "The people will think that we are on your side."

After stopping by the guesthouse to get something to eat and to inform the Lindstedts what was going on, I returned to Tuburan.

That night (Friday), we had a special prayer meeting in the church committing our situation to the Lord and asking Him to intervene for His glory. In the middle of the service, I noticed someone out in the street beckoning for me to come outside. I went out to see what was up.

To my amazement, it was Mr. Alcantara, the former Mayor. He was a Knight of Columbus and an instructor of the Roman Catholic Catechism classes in the public schools. He was the owner of the land in Suba where several of our members were tenants. He had heard me preach several times when we conducted our Saturday night evangelistic meetings in Suba. Though he did not actually attend the meetings, he could hear very clearly what was said and taught as we always used an amplifier. He was the same person who had told the priest that, if he disturbed the grave of Hammer's daughter, he would go to jail. The priest had asked him to accompany him to Cebu City to file a case against us. The priest had thought that he was one of his strong and influential backers. What he did not know was that Mr. Alcantara was one of our sympathizers. He secretly told me everything that had happened in Cebu.

"You had better get 4,000 pesos ready immediately so you can post bond," he advised. "The priest has already had it announced on the radio that you are going to jail."

When I discussed the situation with our leaders, we decided to go to the house of Berting Mercado, the Municipal Secretary. He, too, was a Knight of Columbus but was also proving to be very sympathetic to our cause. When we told him what had happened, he filled us in on other aspects of the plot against us, of which Mr. Alcantara was not aware.

"They're going to pull the old trick," he said.

"What old trick?" I asked.

"They will file the case at 11:45 tomorrow morning (Saturday)." The case will be received and a warrant for the arrest of you and your deacons will be signed. Then the Chief of Police, the Municipal Judge, and the Mayor (all Knights of Columbus) will close their offices for the weekend. No one will be available to accept your bail bond. You will be in jail over the weekend."

When we discovered their plot, the deacons and I decided to leave town immediately so they wouldn't be able to serve the warrants of arrest. Elenor did not want to go with us, as she didn't want to take the boys out on those rough roads at night. I had often left her and the maids alone with the boys when I went on emergency runs.

Elenor could see no reason why they couldn't stay home this time as well. I, however, was nervous about leaving her in this situation, so I rigged up the battery operated amplifier and set it on the dining room table.

"If anything suspicious happens, turn this on and call for help," I instructed. "The Christians will come immediately." By this time, several of our neighbors had accepted Jesus Christ as their Lord and Savior, and I felt certain they could be relied upon to take care of my family.

The three deacons and I then took off for Cebu City. The next morning we were no place to be found in Tuburan, so the plan to arrest us was foiled. When we got to Cebu City, I asked Marv Lindstedt to go to Tuburan to stay with Elenor and to preach for me the following day, which was Sunday. Since the deacons were all with me in hiding, there was no one left in Tuburan who could preach. I also didn't want Elenor to spend another night alone.

In the afternoon a messenger arrived from Tuburan with a letter from Elenor. "Read this for kicks," she wrote, referring to the enclosed letter, which had been delivered to our house. The letter read:

"Mr. Reverend Varbeard,

You have committed a blunder against the Municipal Council and our beloved mayor. Watch out your step. We'll cut off your neck. Remember you are a foreigner in this place.

A sympathizer of the mayor,
Such act is as good as dynamite.
You will see."

When I read the letter, I just laughed. When the deacons saw it, they didn't laugh.

"Do you see the signature?" they asked.

"What signature? There is no signature," I replied.

"Don't you see this red blotch?" they asked. "This letter is signed in blood!"

Sunday afternoon, when Marv arrived back in Cebu City from Tuburan, he told us of how he had been awakened at 4:00 a.m. that morning (Christ the King Sunday for the Catholic Church) by the priest's preaching for four hours about how he was filing a case against us and how he was going to have us put in jail. He called me a "white devil" and used many other adjectives to describe us.

We decided to go back to Tuburan that night. We arrived at about nine o'clock at night. The next morning, I got on my scooter and rode up and down every street in the town. I wanted everyone to know that we were back. I was told later that there was quite a stir around town wondering what would happen to us. I was told that one very devout Catholic lady was asked if she thought those Protestants would dare to go out of their houses after what the priest had done.

"You can't scare those Protestants," she answered. "They're ready to die."

In one sense we were ready to die, but in another we weren't. We still felt that there was much work that needed to be done.

As nine o'clock approached, I kept watching for the arrival of the personnel from the Health Department. Until they arrived, I have to admit, I was becoming a bit anxious. I knew that we would be in a bad situation if they did not keep their promise.

When they did arrive, they drove directly to the Municipal Building. I decided that I should be "as wise as a serpent and as harmless as a dove," as Jesus instructs us. As they got out of their vehicle, I greeted them and publicly informed them that my wife was preparing lunch for them. In Philippine culture, a public invitation given in such a way is very difficult to refuse, so they reluctantly accepted my invitation. This was very important because now they would be staying at my house instead of the priest's house. This, of course, would be of great advantage to our cause!

When the Town Council assembled, the lawyer from the Health Department did his best to persuade the Council to obey the law and establish a Municipal Cemetery. There was much shouting back and forth between the Mayor, the Councilmen, and the officials from the Health Department. One Councilman was particularly skilled in insulting me.

"Why don't these Protestants get their own cemetery instead of expecting us to furnish one for them," he shouted. "I would be the first to give my approval if they need it. Are they so poor they can't even purchase their own lot?"

After much arguing back and forth, the Town Council realized that they would be in deep trouble if they did not obey the law. Finally, one of them said, "Okay, if we are required to establish a Municipal Cemetery, we will. We'll put it right up on top of that mountain!" He pointed to a mountain about seven kilometers away that would be very difficult to climb carrying a coffin.

Just then the lawyer from the Heath Department leaned over to me and said, "Brother, I'm going to see you through this."

I wondered who was calling me "brother." Come to find out, he was the son of Christian parents and had been transferred to Cebu just three weeks previously. He did his best, but the Town Council was very adamant in their stand.

At noon, the Mayor dismissed the Council, and the officials from the Health Department went with me to our house for lunch. As soon as we were seated, Dr. Dy, one of the health officials who had studied in the states, asked if we didn't have any private land that could be used as a Baptist cemetery.

"Yes," I answered, "We have had land for several years but your office has refused to give us the needed approval."

"Well," he said, "We're in charge now. Let's go and see your land."

When we showed him our lot, he smiled and said, "This is a perfect lot for a cemetery. It meets all of the requirements."

He then took a set of application forms from his briefcase and showing them to me stated, "Now, all you have to do is fill these out and have the Mayor and the members of the Town Council sign them. Then bring them to my office and we'll give you a permit."

"That's the problem," I answered. "You saw the Town Council. You know as well as I do that they will not sign anything for us."

"If that is the case, there is nothing I can do," answered Dr. Dy. "The law states that the Town Council must approve the application."

"Listen," I said. "If you don't give us a cemetery today, I am going with you to Cebu City. I will fly directly to Manila to see President Garcia."

The doctor explained that he could do nothing because of the requirements of the law.

Then the lawyer interrupted with a suggestion, "Let's go and see the Mayor right now."

"You can't expect anyone to sign papers that haven't even been filled out," said the doctor.

"Let's go and see," said the lawyer.

Dr. Dy reluctantly agreed and we went to the Mayor's house. When we got there, the lawyer went directly to the Mayor with the papers and handing him a pen, said, "This is where you sign, Sir."

To everyone's amazement, the Mayor took the pen and signed. From there, we went to the councilman's house who had been very vocal in stating that he would be the first to sign if we ever got our own land. I greeted him and informed him that we had our own land and, since he had promised to sign, we had brought the application forms for him to sign.

"I won't sign any papers for you," he stated indignantly.

The lawyer leaned over and whispered something in his ear and again to our amazement, he took the pen and signed! I have often wondered what the lawyer said.

From there, we went to the homes of each Councilman, and since the Mayor and the Chief Councilman had already signed, they signed too!

Seventeen

THE FIRST PROTESTANT CEMETERY

PART THREE

The next step was to go to the Registrar of Deeds in Cebu City. The lawyer from the Health Department offered to go with me. When we entered the office of the Registrar of Deeds, the lawyer handed our application papers to the one in charge and asked him to sign. When that person saw the name "Tuburan Baptist Cemetery," he immediately stated that he could not sign unless we could present a whole list of other required papers. Just then someone whom I had never seen before called me to come out into the hall. I hesitated to go, but he urgently signaled for me to come.

When I went out to meet him, he asked how much money I had spent in that office.

"I haven't spent anything," I answered.

"Then go back in and get your papers and get out of there."

"Why?" I asked.

"Just do as I tell you!"

Not knowing what was up, I decided to obey. When I got back in the hall, the man introduced himself as an attorney, a friend of Roy Nelson's, who was a BGC missionary living in Bogo. He had overheard what we were trying to accomplish and knew the secrets of getting papers processed in that office.

"Are you trying to register donated land as a cemetery?" he asked.

"Yes," I answered.

"You'll never make it if it is donated land," he explained. "Go back to Tuburan and change all of your papers. Buy the land for one peso and then come back."

I followed his advice, and two days later, I was back with a deed of sale for the property. When I presented this to the lady who was then at the desk, she looked it over and explained that we still lacked the incorporation papers of the Tuburan Baptist Church. I calmly explained that the Tuburan Church was not yet incorporated but that it was a member church of the Baptist Conference of the Philippines, which is incorporated. As we talked, she asked me if I knew Roy Nelson and the Baptist missionaries in Bogo.

"Yes," I said, "we are with the same mission."

"Then I am going to help you," she said with a smile.

With that, she immediately began processing our papers. Come to find out, she was from Bogo and was sympathetic to our cause. Within only a few minutes, our papers were complete and I was heading for the Regional Health Department. The lawyer from the Regional Health Department once again agreed to help by going with me to the Provincial Health Office to get the signature of Dr. Laborte, the director.

"The Provincial Health Office is under our regional office," he explained. "I'll just go with you to make sure that Dr. Laborte signs."

When we got to the Provincial Health Office, the attorney took the papers directly to Dr. Laborte's desk.

"I am the attorney for the Regional Office," he said. "We have checked over all of these papers and everything is in order. Just sign here, please."

When Dr. Laborte saw "Tuburan Baptist Cemetery," he just brushed the papers aside saying, "I don't have to sign any papers!"

"But, Sir, we have checked them over at the regional office. Everything is in order."

"I don't care who has checked them over. I don't have to sign. What's more I am busy. Come back in the morning." He then proceeded to insult the lawyer.

At this point, the lawyer was both angry and insulted.

"I give up!" he said, as we walked out of the office. "I'm not going back to that guy again!"

Well, I wasn't ready to give up. At 8 o'clock the following morning, I was again in Dr. Laborte's office. When he saw me, he glared at me and said, "I don't have any time to see you about any Protestant cemetery. I have 150 doctors coming in today and I don't have time for you!"

"Okay," I resolutely answered, "I am also a busy man, so I will just sit here until you do have time."

With that, I sat down on a chair right in front of his desk. It turned out that he was telling the truth. There were about 150 doctors coming in that morning. As they each came into the office, they each very politely asked me if they could help me in any way.

"No," I answered, "I am just waiting for Dr. Laborte to sign some papers." This went on over and over again from 8 a.m. to 11:45 a.m. Finally, Dr. Laborte got so frustrated with me and so embarrassed that he took out his pen and signed our papers.

"Now get out of here!" he shouted.

I was very glad to accommodate him. I rushed out to my car and raced down the street to the Regional Health Office. I arrived just as Dr. Dy was coming out of his office to go for lunch. I handed him the signed papers.

"You mean to tell me that you have all of the papers signed?" he asked in amazement.

"Yes," I answered, "I believe they are all complete."

He looked them over and then went back into his office.

"You have accomplished more in a few days than can usually be accomplished in several years," he exclaimed "but I'm going to sign them too." With that, he took out his pen and signed.

As I walked out of his office, I could hardly believe what God had done. We now had the first Protestant cemetery that I was aware of in the whole Province of Cebu.

When I got back to Tuburan, the Christians were overjoyed that we now had our own cemetery. I told the members to spread the word around town that it was open to all religions free of charge.

Shortly after that, a Roman Catholic member died and the family went to the priest to ask permission to bury in the Catholic cemetery. The priest agreed provided they pay the usual fifty pesos. The family refused to pay, explaining that if he demanded payment, they were going to bury in the Baptist cemetery. The priest would not budge, so they buried in our cemetery. When the priest thought over what had transpired, he really became angry! He realized that now one of his chief sources of income was in jeopardy.

The priest then decided that now more than ever he needed to make sure that we landed in jail. He had already announced that he would charge us with trespassing, offending religious feelings, and several other offences. When he consulted with his lawyers, however, they informed him that the only charge that had any possibility of success was the charge of offending religious feelings. There, too, the possibility of success was very small. In the end, he decided that perhaps it was best just to drop the charges.

When this happened, the leaders of the Catholic church were embarrassed. They felt they had lost face. They went to the priest and told him that since he had announced on the radio and also over his public address system that he was going to put us in jail, he had better keep his word or they would stop coming to his church.

First Protestant Cemetery –
Tuburan Cemetery

As a result, the priest decided to push through with his case. I then had the word spread around town that whoever signed the case against us had better think twice, as we would be forced to file counter charges.

The local judge decided that he didn't want to sign the case, so he sent the papers to the chief of police. The chief of police didn't want to sign so he sent them back to the judge. This sending of the papers from one office to another went on for several weeks.

During those weeks, I was called into the municipal building several times and threatened with a jail sentence. Nothing happened, however, until one day, the judge (the Grand Knight of Columbus) called me to his office.

"I'm being forced to sign these papers against you," he said. "I am, however, embarrassed to sign them and to issue a warrant for your arrest. Now here is what I will do. I will give you and the six members, who are also being charged along with you, until Monday to prepare a bail bond of 7,000 pesos. Then, after you have posted your bonds, I will issue the warrant for your arrests. In this way you won't have to go to jail because your bond will already be posted."

I was amazed at the response of our members when they receive this news.

"We have done nothing wrong," they said. "We will not post any bond. If they want to arrest us, let them go right ahead."

"Don't worry," I said. "I will post the bond for you."

On the advice of Attorney Aliño, I was carrying in my pocket at all times a bail bond for 4,000 pesos that I had purchased from a bonding company in Cebu City. All I would have to do was fill in the number of the case and I would be free on bail. The members explained that they were not posting bond, and they were not allowing a bond to be posted for them.

"We have done what we have done for our Lord and we are not ashamed of it," was their united stand.

Following their stand, I, too, decided not to post bond. I went to the Municipal Building to inform the Municipal Secretary of our decision. The ex-mayor and the vice-mayor were both standing there and heard what I had said. They immediately stepped forward and offered to post bond for us.

"No," I said, "We are not posting bond and we are not accepting bond. Furthermore, I want to inform you that when we are arrested we will be ready. I will bring my camera, my Bible, my songbook, and my public addressP.A. system. We will hold services right here in your jail. Besides that," I continued, "I will send three telegrams: one to the *Time Magazine*, one to *The Free Press*, and one to the American Embassy explaining what is happening."

"Wait just a minute," exclaimed the municipal secretary. "We'd better go to see the Mayor."

"Okay," I said, "Let's go."

When we arrived at the Mayor's residence, we explained what had happened. I told him what my plans were. For the first time, the mayor (also a Knight of Columbus) decided to take a stand against the priest.

"Don't you do anything," he instructed. "I'll take care of that priest."

The result was that the priest was forced to drop the case. Some of his loyal fanatical members, however, tried to find a way for him to save face.

One day, one of them came to our house with the following confession they wanted us to sign.

"We, the undersigned, after proper deliberation, hereby declare and make manifest:

That we admit that we read the scriptures and sang hymns in connection with the burial of the dead body of a Child, _____, at the Roman Catholic Cemetery;

That we did all these in the belief that they are not the acts referred to as punishable under Art. 133, particularly, or the Revised Penal Code;

That, in spite of anything, prompted by our desire for peace and goodwill, fearing that said acts although may not be criminal as believed by some people, we solemnly and earnestly beg that we be forgiven for any unthought of consequences of said actuations of ours by people concerned;

That this is done by us with the trust and confidence that this may not be used against us in any way, particularly in connection with or in relation to any charge, civil or criminal, which may be filed against us.

Done at Tuburan, Cebu, Philippines, this ____ day of December, 1960."

I, of course, refused to sign this confession. I did, however, keep a copy as evidence of their plots, just in case I might need it later. As a result of all of the above experiences, the members of the Tuburan church became more and more convinced that "If the Lord be for us, who can be against us." So did I.

Eighteen

A SUBPOENA IS ISSUED

In early 1961, Andy Nelson and his family settled in Balamban to begin missionary work there. This was only about an hour's drive south of Tuburan, and they became our closest missionary neighbors. After they settled, they began reaching out to the surrounding community. After a few months , Andy decided that it was time to conduct an evangelistic tent crusade. He set up a large tent on a rented lot and asked Pastor Batuto, an excellent evangelist and chalk artist, and others to help him.

From the first night, the attendance was great. Several hundred people attended each night. This created no small stir in the town, and the priest became very concerned. To create confusion and, hopefully, to put an end to the meetings, he organized his followers into a religious procession. Each night, they would march round and round the tent, carrying lighted candles, singing and chanting.

Andy didn't know what to do so he drove up to Tuburan to ask my advice.

"What can we do?" asked Andy. "We can't even hear inside the tent."

After thinking about the situation, I advised Andy to have his camera ready the next night to take pictures of the priest and those in procession with him. Andy followed my advice and took several pictures that night. The following morning, a policeman showed up at Andy's door ordering him to come to the office of the chief of Police. Andy did not go but went instead to Cebu City to have his film developed.

When Andy got back to Balamban, the policeman returned—this time with a subpoena. Since he had a subpoena, Andy agreed to go with him to the office of the chief of Police. There, he found the Chief of Police and the priest waiting for him.

"You have been charged with offending religious feelings! You have been charged with taking pictures of this priest while he was performing religious ceremonies! Are these charges true? If they are, what can you say in your defense? Why would you do such a thing?" asked the Chief of Police.

"I took pictures of the priest because my legal counsel advised me to do so. I was advised to take pictures so that I would have legal proof that the priest was trespassing on our property and interrupting our religious services," answered Andy.

"Do you have pictures? Can you prove this?"

"Yes," answered Andy. "I have pictures and I can prove that the priest and his companions were trespassing."

Thereupon, the chief asked to see the pictures. When he saw the pictures, the Chief of Police decided that they should all go to the site and make an on-site verification of the charges. Upon examining the boundaries of the mission-rented property, it became evident that the priest was indeed the trespasser.

"Under the circumstances would you like to continue the case?" asked the Chief as he turned to the priest.

"No, I'll guess I'll drop the case," answered the cornered priest.

That same August, a man appeared at our door seeking help. He introduced himself as a Christian tenant farmer living south of Balamban. He had heard of me and hoped that I would help him. His landlord had ordered him off his property when he had become a Protestant. He, however, had stood on his constitutional rights and refused to move. The landlord had then filed a false charge of theft against him—accusing him of stealing five dollars' worth of firewood. It is, of course, the right of a tenant farmer to gather firewood from the land he is farming.

I did my best to help this farmer and went with him to discuss the case with the judge in that town. The judge turned out to be very prejudiced against Protestants. Hoping to encourage him to follow the law, I let him know that I would be backing my Christian brother and observing how he handled the case.

Fortunately, when I introduced this defendant to Attorney Aliño in Cebu City, he volunteered to take the case and defend him. As Attorney Aliño feared, the case was lost in the local municipal court, but he appealed the case to a higher court, and the case went on for many years. Cases like this were common in those days. Becoming a Protestant was no small decision.

> *"They will deliver you to synagogues and prisons, and you will be brought before kings and governors, and all on account of my name. This will result in your being witnesses to them. But make up your mind not to worry beforehand how you will defend yourselves. For I will give you words and wisdom that none of your adversaries will be able to resist or contradict. You will be betrayed even by parents, brothers, relatives and friends, and they will put some of you to death. All men will hate you because of me. But not a hair of your head will perish. By standing firm you will gain life."*
> *(Luke 21:12-19)*

Nineteen

SEA URCHINS

A survey trip of Leyte in 1963 proved to be a very memorable trip for me. It was not only an opportunity to see many unreached areas that seemed very open to the gospel, but also a great time of fellowship with my fellow missionaries. Several incidents stick clearly in my mind and I have often enjoyed telling them.

We decided to use the boat of missionary George Chalmers' who was then living in Cataingan, Masbate. This boat, called *The Good News*, was a typical thirty-foot Leyte-type outrigger canoe, except for the few refinements George had made. These included a plywood-covered portion in the bow under which we could store our luggage and on which we could sit or lie down. There was also a removable canvas roof. He had installed a Briggs and Stratton engine (9 hp) as an inboard engine. There was also a Johnson Outboard (25 hp) at the rear. The boat moved well in the water, and we could travel at a good speed if we used both engines.

We first headed for Gingatangan Island to visit Pastor Batuto. He had gone to school in Bogo, Cebu, and while living there, had been converted under the ministry of Andrew Nelson and Irwin Bjelland. He later felt called to the ministry and had gone on to get pastoral training at the Far Eastern Bible Institute and Seminary (FEBIAS) in Manila. He became a very gifted evangelistic chalk artist and served in many of the tent campaigns that were conducted by our mission. When not serving as an evangelist, he would go home to Gingatangan and pastor the church he had established there.

Gingatangan is one of the islands included in the province of Leyte and is a very flat. I doubt that any portion of the island is over thirty feet above sea level. It looked very small and insignificant as we approached—especially with the high mountains of Naval Island in the background. There is no deep-water port on the island, so as we drew near to the island, Pastor Nueva, who had decided to accompany us, grabbed a long bamboo pole and stood at the bow of our boat and watched for rocks. When he saw that we were heading directly towards one, he reached out with his pole to push us away from the rock. The rock proved to be very slippery, however, and as he pushed, the pole slipped, and Nueva went head first into the ocean. When this happened, we were all laughing so hard that we had difficulty pulling him back on board. When the

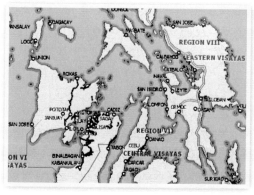

Map of Central Philippines

water became too shallow to go any farther, we dropped several anchors and waded ashore. We had a delightful fellowship with Pastor and Mrs. Batuto and their members and, of course, they served us something to eat. We saw the beautiful A-frame church building they had erected, as well as a lovely parsonage.

As the afternoon wore on, we decided that it was time for us to be on our way, as we planned to spend the night in Naval. Pastor Batuto encouraged us to just borrow some of the small canoes that were plentiful on the beach and row out in them to our anchored boat.

"The owners won't mind and that way you won't get wet," he advised.

Andy Nelson and Jerry Osbron were the first to go in one of the canoes. This canoe was too small for the two of them. In spite of this, Andy began deliberately rocking the canoe from side to side. Jerry was infuriated and yelled for him to stop. All of us on shore laughed as we watched this duel. It was so out of character for Andy to do such a thing! Suddenly, one of the outriggers broke and all we could see were two arms sticking up out of the water—each holding a camera. How we laughed as we watched the two of them scramble to get back onto the slippery overturned canoe. When they finally made it, they rode the canoe as though it were a horse!

We then heard Andy complaining that he had lost his shoes. Jerry, who is a good swimmer, graciously volunteered to find them. He gave Andy his camera and dove in.

"I see them," he yelled as his head popped up out of the water. "I'll get them."

Thereupon he dove down again. What he had seen were not shoes, however, but sea urchins! He grabbed them with his hands and then, when he realized his mistake, kicked strongly to get away and ended up kicking both feet into other urchins! He came to the surface groaning in pain. We quickly assisted him back to the shore. He must have had between thirty and fifty broken quills in his hands and feet! Those who have had even one quill in one of their feet know how painful these poisonous quills can be.

None of us missionaries had had much experience with sea urchins and didn't know what to do. Mrs. Batuto, however, came running and offered advice.

"Just urinate on them and the pain will go away," she said.

Jerry was unconvinced and wanted to be immediately transported to the doctor in Naval. This we did and Jerry had a rather lengthy stay on the doctor's table as he laboriously tried to extract the quills one at a time. We later learned that Mrs. Batuto's advice should have been followed. The acid in urine does readily neutralize the poison contained in the quills.

While in Naval, we were informed that the local Catholic priest, Father John, was an American. We decided to visit him. When we arrived at his home, he cordially invited us in. We spent some time discussing the local situation with him.

After some time, I decided to probe a bit. "What do you have to say about your church, the Catholic Church, here in the Philippines?"

Father John thought a bit and then answered: "There are two things that amaze me about our church. The first is how little has been accomplished in 400 years. The second is that the people still call themselves Roman Catholics."

I think the reaction of Father John to his church in the Philippines is a common reaction of many Americans. Some may even say that Filipinos aren't true Roman Catholics. The question I ask is, who are the true Roman Catholics, the Filipinos or the Americans?

As I have traveled around the world, I have observed that the practices of the Roman Catholics in the Philippines are much more similar to those practiced in Latin American and Europe than are the practices of Roman Catholics in the United States. Roman Catholics in the United States have absorbed many Protestant practices, and this makes American Roman Catholics quite different from Roman Catholics in Italy and most other Roman Catholic countries. Perhaps this is why American bishops are often at odds with edicts coming from Rome.

Twenty

GOD PROVES THE GOVERNOR WRONG

When we first surveyed Masbate Province, we paid a
visit to the governor's office. The governor received us
very cordially. One thing he wanted to know was what we planned to do if
we opened a mission in Masbate.

I informed him that amongst other things we hoped the missionary assigned
there would be able to buy a lot and build a church.

"You mean to tell me that your mission plans to buy a lot here in Masbate
City on which to build a Protestant Church?"

"Yes," I answered.

"You'll never succeed," was his rather curt response.

"Why not?" I asked.

"There is no one in this town who will sell you a lot for a Protestant
church."

With that response, I wondered if Masbate would be just as difficult for us
to evangelize as Cebu had been.

The Chesbros were the first missionaries from our mission assigned to
Masbate City. Three years later, Elenor and I were assigned to replace them. I
had not lived in Masbate City long before I realized the importance of secur-
ing a church site and building our own respectable church building. Without
these, the spread of the gospel throughout the province would be greatly
hindered. I did not feel, however, that I should make our search for a church

site public knowledge. I feared the opposition would frighten any possible sellers. I did pray diligently, however, that God would provide the lot of His choice at His time.

I often went to the tennis court, which was near our house to get some exercise and to make friends with the players. I soon became friends with Mr. Sarti, the Provincial Engineer. One day, I asked him if he had a map of the city showing all of the existing buildings.

"Yes, I do," he answered.

"Could I get a copy of it?" I asked.

"Yes, of course, provided you pay to have a blueprint made."

"I will be most happy to pay for it," I answered.

When I got the map, I began studying the layout of the city. I noted where the schools, the government buildings, the major businesses, and the market were located. As I studied the map, I prayed that God would impress upon my mind where he wanted His church located. As I continued to study and pray, one particular block surrounded by Mabini, Ibañez, Quezon, and Danao Streets stood out as the most strategic location for our church. I talked to no one about this, except the Lord.

Then one day, Fausto Bayot, another tennis court friend, paid me a visit. He was a member of one of the most prominent Spanish families in town. His father had been one of the first governors of the province.

"Reverend, would you be interested in buying a house and lot?" he asked.

"I might be," I answered. "It depends on where they are located."

"Come. Hop in the car and I will show you."

To my amazement, he drove directly to the block I had been praying for and showed me his house and lot. The house was a large Spanish-type house that could easily be remodeled into a worship center with an adjoining parsonage. Another area being used as a gambling den with a storefront could also be converted into a youth center. The lot was 921 square meters in size and was surrounded by a hollow block fence. I could hardly believe my eyes!

"As you know," Fausto clarified, "I'm building this new hotel and theater complex. Frankly, I'm running out of funds. Attorney Manlapas, the attorney presently living on the premises, has already offered me 35,000 pesos for the property but I thought I would give you a chance to also make a bid on it."

I told Fausto that I would need time to pray about it and to discuss the situation with the mission. He agreed to give me a little time. When I shared the possibility with the members of the church, everyone was very excited. They thought it was an excellent location and a reasonable price, but saw no way that they could raise the necessary amount. They were, however, will-

Bayot house converted into chapel
– Masbate Church, 1965

ing to invest all of the funds the church had been saving up for the purchase of property. They were also willing to commit the church to paying off a loan for the remainder, if a loan could be negotiated from someone with reasonable interest. Johnny Miller, a local businessman and rancher whose grandfather was an American, handed me 1,000 pesos and encouraged us to buy the property. I asked everyone to make this a real matter of prayer.

When I called Irv Bjelland, the mission treasurer, he quickly pointed out that there was nothing in the budget for a church site in Masbate. He did, however, state that, in the past, the mission board had always done everything it could to help in situations like this if there was agreement among the missionaries on the field and a good case could be made for the project.

The more I thought about the issue, the more I became convinced that God wanted us to have the property. It was located in the exact block that I had been praying for! I had never mentioned to Fausto that we were looking for a lot and yet he had come to me.

After several days of praying about the matter, I went to see Fausto. I told him that I was convinced that God wanted us to have the property but that at present we did not have the money. I did, however, offer him 30,000 pesos for the property. I told him that I could give a small down payment and the remainder within three months.

"Thirty thousand pesos? I told you that Attorney Manlapas has already offered 35,000," exclaimed Fausto in surprise.

"Yes, I know, but 30,000 is all that we can afford and I believe that God wants us to have the property for His church," I answered with conviction.

To make a long story short, a few days later, Fausto informed me that he would accept our offer. Irv Bjelland was right—the mission board agreed to give the money to the Baptist General Conference Philippine Mission, and the Philippine Mission agreed to give a loan to the Masbate Baptist Church. The money came from "Lift" funds. "Lift" was a special fundraising program in which the Baptist General Conference was involved at that time. How we rejoiced in this very clear answer to our prayers!

When Attorney Manlapas heard that we had bought the property for less than he had offered, he was very angry. He looked for several months for a place to move his family. Eventually, he ended up purchasing George Ng's Bakery where our church had previously been meeting.

The above-mentioned lot was our first lot in Masbate City. When we left Masbate in 1997, we owned sixteen lots in that city, and the last one was donated by one of the succeeding governors! God seems to love to do the things we think cannot be done! I am reminded of the words of a chorus we used to sing:

> "Got any rivers you think are un-crossable,
> Got any mountains you can't tunnel through,
> God specializes in things thought impossible,
> And He can do what no other friend can do."

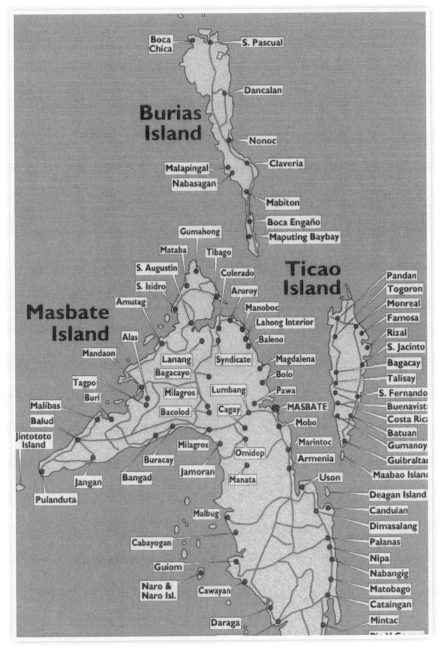

Masbate Province

97

Twenty-One

A TORNADO AT SEA

One day in September of 1965, George Chalmers and I took time out of our busy schedules to survey Ticao Island. Ticao is visible from our house and ever since our arrival in Masbate, I had wondered how many people lived there and if anyone was reaching them with the gospel. We loaded my Zundapp motor scooter into a large motorized outrigger canoe that sailed to Ticao each morning. This canoe was used for commercial purposes and was over thirty feet long. The hull was made from a large hollowed out log and the part extending above the water was constructed of half-inch marine plywood. It could accommodate over fifty passengers or a truckload of *copra* (the meat of the coconut). Boats constructed in this way are very sea-worthy and after having been caught in many a storm sailing between the islands, I have developed more confidence in outrigger canoes than in any flat-bottomed boat—especially when the seas are rough.

The trip to the island was uneventful and took only about an hour and a half. From the number of passengers that accompanied us, it was obvious that there was much commerce between Masbate and Ticao. We were informed that Ticao is actually a part of Masbate province.

As we approached the island, we gazed at an exceedingly picturesque scene. Many fishermen were coming home in their little one-man canoes—some with sails, some paddling. On the shore were children playing in the sand. Some were swimming out to meet their fathers who were bringing home the night's catch. They hoped the catch was good, so that some of it could be sold in the market to raise money to support their families' many needs and maybe even buy some candy. Nearby both men and women mended their fishing nets under the coconut trees. It was a peaceful scene, and I couldn't help but wonder if these people had peace in their hearts.

We unloaded the motor scooter and began riding down the only road on the island. It led up over the mountain range that runs down the center of the island and then followed the northeastern coastline. Though the road was very poor and the bridges primitive, we were able to make good progress. Both George and I marveled at the beauty of the island. The white beaches covered with tall coconut trees interspersed with picturesque Nipa huts built on stilts made us regret that we hadn't brought our cameras. Certainly, one could take a prize-winning picture here that the *National Geographic* or some similar magazine would be glad to purchase.

That day, we visited many *barrios* (villages) and four towns. We found the economy very similar to that of Masbate. Fishing, rice farming, and coconut harvesting were the main sources of income. We were told that there was one very large cattle ranch in the south, though we weren't able to go there. The language was very similar to that of Masbate, and we could converse freely with the people. They seemed very friendly. We noticed that some were of lighter skin than most Filipinos. We were told that this was because Ticao had been the jumping off place for Spanish schooners during the Spanish regime. From Ticao they would sail through the San Bernadino Straits and on to Mexico. Apparently, many of these sailors found the local girls attractive and left many sons and daughters behind.

When we questioned the people about their religion, we found that most professed to be Roman Catholics. We were able to find only one Protestant chapel on the whole island. This chapel was very dilapidated, and it was easy to see the sky through the holes in the Nipa palm shingles. As we questioned the people nearby, it was obvious that very little, if any, gospel was being preached. The government officials informed us that there were 95,000 people living on Ticao.

After reaching the end of the road, George and I headed back to the village where we had disembarked that morning. When we arrived we found the same canoe waiting for us. We loaded the scooter and were climbing on board when I happened to look up at the sky.

"Look at that sky!" I exclaimed to George. There was a very black streak running across the sky north of us.

"Ah, that's nothing," George answered. George was a lover of the sea and had been in the U.S. Navy during World War II. He knew much more about the sea and ocean travel than I did, so I relaxed and forgot about the strange looking clouds.

As we sailed towards home, George and I discussed the situation of the people of Ticao. We both were heavily burdened by what we had found. To think that there were 95,000 people living so near to us who were still ignorant of the gospel! Though we both already felt overloaded with responsibilities, we knew that something must be done to reach the people of Ticao with the gospel.

What bothered us even more was our knowledge that Ticao was only one of many unreached islands. There were so many islands and so few were really being reached! Even Masbate Island, where missionaries had already worked for several years still had many whole counties with no gospel witness. What could we do? How could we operate more efficiently? How could we spread the gospel more rapidly?

These questions had often kept me awake at night. There were so many open doors—so many people going to a lost eternity! Why were so few missionaries being appointed? If only the people back home could understand. If only they would catch a vision of what could be accomplished if the whole church of Jesus Christ were mobilized to spread the gospel!

Sometimes it almost seemed that we were placed in the position of God—deciding who would get the gospel and have a chance to go to heaven. It is easy for a missionary to say "yes" to one area, until he or she realizes that by saying "yes" to one area, he or she is actually saying "no" to others. There just aren't enough workers to go around. And then to realize that every day many people are dying without ever hearing God's wonderful message of life! Why doesn't the church wake up? Why are there so few missionaries coming out?

As questions like these were going through my mind, I looked up just in time to see it!

"Look out!" I shouted.

I saw something black coming towards us accompanied by a terrific roar! I felt myself being deluged with water. I could hear bamboo breaking. The wind was tremendous! I remember placing my hand in front of my face and seeing only a faint shadow.

Suddenly, there was dead silence for a few seconds. Then the roar, the water, the wind again! I heard a crash, and felt a shudder run through the boat. Then it was over. Within moments, the sun was shining.

We found ourselves near the shore of Masbate. The water was only shoulder deep. Our boat had hit a submerged rock. The canvas roof was gone. The propeller was broken. The drive shaft was bent. But we were safe! Both the boat and we had miraculously survived.

What had happened? The people on the shore told us that they had seen it. "It was a *bujawi*" (a waterspout), they said. It had even ripped some of the galvanized steel sheets off the roofs of houses. "The sheets went straight up into the air!" they exclaimed in wonderment.

What I have never been able to understand is how we got from the center of the Ticao Straits to the shore of Masbate. Whether we were blown very rapidly across the water, or whether we were actually lifted completely out of the water, I will never know. I do know that the dead silence we experienced for a couple of seconds in the middle of the whole affair must have been the eye of the tornado. It's highly possible, from what I have read about similar storms, that we were actually carried through the air! I was once again reminded that God must have miraculously saved George and me for a purpose. Certainly, reaching the people of Ticao with the gospel must be part of that purpose. Could it also be that the devil didn't want us invading his territory and had attempted to wipe us out?

> *"If you make the Most High your dwelling—even the LORD, who is my refuge—no disaster will come near your tent. For he will command his angels concerning you to guard you in all your ways; they will lift you up in their hands, so that you will not strike your foot against a stone." (Psa. 91:9-12)*

Twenty-Two

THANK GOD FOR CHICKENS

One week in 1966, we and the Chalmers were trying to figure out how we could get to the Field Council meeting in Cebu City that was to begin on Monday afternoon. There were no direct flights from Masbate to Cebu and there were no ships leaving Sunday afternoon or evening. We finally decided that my wife, Elenor, and Nancy Chalmers, together with the kids, should take the *Agustina* on Friday night. The *Agustina* was a World War II vintage ship that regularly plied the Masbate-Cebu route. Since our mission work was still new in Masbate, neither George nor I had anyone trained who could preach for us on Sunday mornings. We both felt that we must stay for the weekend at our respective posts—He in Cataingan and I in Masbate City. The plan was that George would then come to Masbate City on Monday morning and, hopefully, we would catch connecting flights, and eventually end up in Cebu by Monday evening.

On Monday morning, I packed my bags in preparation for the trip to Cebu and waited for George to arrive from Cataingan. After waiting for some time, I concluded that something must have gone wrong. I decided to go to the bus depot just in case George had decided to take the bus. When the bus from Cataignan arrived, it was filled with people, but I looked in vain for George. It seemed apparent that he was not on board until the conductor opened the bodega. The bodega is a space at the back of the bus for pigs and chickens. To my amazement out came George and several other people. He looked rather peaked and a little green.

"Hey, how was the trip?" I asked with a grin.

"Oh, not too bad," he answered.

"You mean to tell me no one was vomiting back there?"

"Oh yea, several were vomiting," George answered, "but thank God there were enough chickens to eat it up!"

"Well, come on. Let's go to the house. You're not riding on the plane with me until you've had a shower. You smell like a sick pig!"

On the way to the house, George explained what had happened. He left Cataingan early in the morning as planned. When he reached the first river, he discovered that the bridge had been washed out. His only option was to leave his vehicle at a neighboring farmhouse and wade across the river where he had a choice of riding on one of two waiting buses.

After he had boarded one of the buses, the two drivers began racing each other. Sure enough, the one on which George was riding broke down. This, of course, was what the other bus driver had hoped for so he would then get all of the passengers! At this point, George was at a disadvantage. Being a long-legged six foot three, it took him some time to untangle his legs from between the wooden benches and get out of the first bus. By the time he reached the second bus, it was already full. This meant that he had only two options: ride in the bodega or walk. He chose the bodega. It was an uncomfortable ride, but he made it.

After George had cleaned up, we went to the airport. We were just in time to catch the plane for Calbayog, Samar—an old Douglas DC3. DC3s were the standard planes used on the undeveloped grass landing strips that were common in many areas of the Philippines at that time.

In about thirty minutes, we disembarked on another grass strip in Calbayog, Samar. We looked for the terminal building and decided that the small run-down-looking shack at the edge of the runway must be it. When we inquired about our connecting flight to Tacloban, Leyte, we were assured that it would be arriving soon. We saw no place to sit down in the terminal building, so we sat down under a tree on the edge of the runway and watched the water buffalo grazing on the airstrip.

In about an hour, we heard a plane in the distance. The airport personnel came running out to chase the water buffalo off the runway. We were glad the plane was on time, as this would give us a good chance of catching our connecting flight from Tacloban to Cebu. To our disappointment, however, it began raining just as the plane was coming in for a landing. The pilot apparently felt that it was unsafe to

Riding with the governor (first on left) in a DC3 with no seats

land, so he pulled back on the stick and, flopping his wings, flew off into the distance.

"Now what do we do?" I asked.

We walked over to a man who looked intelligent and asked for advice. He informed us that we could still get to Cebu.

"All you need to do is walk down this road about a mile to the crossing," he volunteered. "If you wait there for about an hour, there will be a bus heading for Catbalogan. Take that and you will be in Catbalogan tonight in time to catch the ship going to Tacloban. If you ride that ship all night, you will be in Tacloban the following morning. From there you can catch a bus to Ormoc City where you can catch another ship that evening for Cebu. You will be in Cebu the following morning."

George and I realized that following his advice would probably get us to Cebu but that the Field Council would already be over. George had another idea.

"Come on Dick," he said. "Let's go down to the pier and see what's in port."

We flagged down a tricycle (a 100cc motorcycle with a sidecar) and climbed aboard. When we got to the port area, we saw various vessels either loading or unloading cargo. One was an old wooden launch piled high with sacks of copra that looked like it was preparing to leave. *Copra* is the dried meat of the coconut.

"Where are you going?" George called out in the local dialect.

"Cebu," was the answer.

"How long will the trip take?"

"Only about eighteen hours," was the answer.

George and I talked it over and decided that, though it would get us to Cebu a day late, it was probably the best we could do.

"Could we possibly ride along?" George asked. "We need to get to Cebu as soon as possible,"

"You want to ride with us?" the man asked with an amazed look on his face.

"Yes, we do," George and I answered in unison.

"Come on aboard," the man answered and held out his hand to assist us up a wooden plank that served as a gangplank.

George and I looked around and discovered that the only sleeping accommodations would be to find a comfortable spot and nestle down between sacks of copra. Though George didn't like the idea very much, we began moving the sacks around to make our beds.

"How soon are we leaving?" we asked.

"Immediately," was the answer.

"I wish we would have had enough time to buy some food," I said regretfully.

"Oh these guys must be eating something," George said. "They won't let us starve."

In similar situations, generous Filipinos had often fed both George and me. Filipinos are so hospitable they never eat in the presence of anyone without offering to share whatever they have. They always offer a visitor the best portion.

As we watched, we saw several members of the crew go down into the hold to start the engine. We heard several strange sounds but no sound of an engine starting. After about half an hour, a very greasy man appeared, carrying a starter.

"The starter is broken," he said, and walked down the gangplank and headed towards what appeared to be some sort of repair shop down the road.

George and I waited and wondered what would go wrong next. After about an hour, the man came walking back with a grin on his face and proudly stated, "I got it fixed!" We were thankful and watched him disappear into the hold.

After about half an hour, we heard them attempting once again to start the engine. This time it started and a huge column of black smoke arose from the exhaust stack. Then there was another bang and clang and another engine started.

"Hey," I said, "This thing has two engines!"

The ropes anchoring the launch to the pier were soon loosened, and we began to back away from the pier. At the proper time, the captain rang the bell signaling the engine room to shift into forward gear and open the throttles to full speed ahead. George and I looked at each other in disappointment as we saw that despite the huge amount of smoke coming out of the smoke stacks, we were only making about four knots an hour.

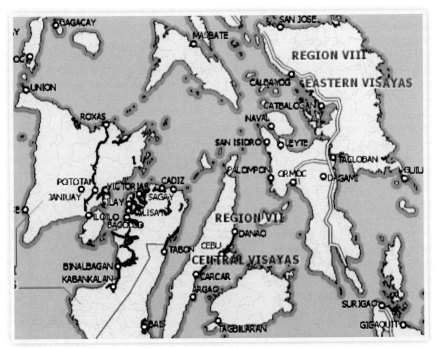

Map of Central Philippines

Trying to give our situation a positive twist, I turned to George and said, "Just think what people back in the states would give for a beautiful ocean cruise like this!" George grinned, but didn't look too impressed.

When we were only about one hour into our journey, there was a bang in the engine room and one engine stopped. Now we were down to two knots an hour! Then about an hour later, the other engine also stopped and we were dead in the water!

George had worked in the engine room of a navy ship, and I saw him disappear down the ladder leading to the engine room. A few minutes later, he reappeared.

"Come on Dick," he urged, "they're both Caterpillar engines, and what broke on one didn't break on the other. I think we can get one engine going again."

George was right, and before long, we were again "cruising" along at two knots an hour. It was getting dark and a beautiful moon was coming up over the waters. I looked up at the stars and marveled at the beauty of God's creation. Traveling among the 7,000 islands of the Philippines on a moonlit night can be a most aesthetic experience! I moved some of the sacks of copra around a bit until I had a comfortable spot and was soon fast asleep.

"Dick, where is the flashlight?" was the sound that awakened me some time later.

"Shut up and go to sleep," I answered.

"No, I need the flashlight," George pled.

George soon found it without my help.

"Look!" he exclaimed as he shined the light on himself.

I looked and saw that George's body was one gray moving mass! He had decided to sleep on an open space of the wooden deck instead of on the sacks of copra. During the cool of the night, the copra maggots had left their hiding places and crawled out onto the deck where they discovered George!

George began beating his clothes in an attempt to remove the hundreds of maggots. Maggots were flying in every direction! I laughed until my sides almost burst as I watched George dance around trying to free himself from his visitors! Needless to say, George spent the remainder of the night up on the sacks of copra beside me. I heard him scratching away before I fell back to sleep. I'm not sure how much he slept that night.

The next morning, the sun rose beautifully over the eastern horizon. It wasn't long, however, until hunger pangs were visiting both George and me. We noticed that everyone had gone below deck so we decided to do the same. As we expected, the crew was eating breakfast. They had lit a small charcoal fire over which they were roasting some tiny dried fish and some ears of dry corn. They were somewhat embarrassed that we had caught them eating such simple food. Their cultural habit of hospitality, however, forced them to offer us whatever they had, and we were glad to accept. It's amazing how hunger makes even the simplest of meals taste mighty good!

After breakfast, George and I went back up on deck. I always felt a little queasy in the hold of a ship even if the seas were calm. The diesel fumes mixed with the smell of dried fish and copra usually sent my stomach for a spin. George often accused me of having a weak stomach.

When we got topside, it was already getting very hot. The only shade we could find was to huddle close to the shady side of the little wooden cockpit that served as the bridge. We were moving so slowly in the water that we wondered if we would ever reach Cebu City. The captain told us not to worry. "The owner always sends another launch to pull us back to port if we have trouble," he assured us.

Having nothing else to do, I suggested to George that I call the meeting to order. I was the chairman of the Property Committee and George was one of the two other members. "Anyway, we already have a quorum," I declared with a grin. We discussed several of our agenda items, but it was so hot we had difficulty concentrating. By midday, we were running parallel with the Cebu coastline about a mile off shore. We were still a long ways from Cebu City. We could see buses passing by along the coastal road heading for Cebu City. How we wished we could somehow get ashore.

Before I realized it, George had disappeared. When he reappeared he had a grin on his face. He had been down in the hold snooping around.

"There's an old dugout canoe down in the hold. Let's see if we can talk the captain into letting us use it," he suggested.

The captain couldn't imagine what we wanted with the old canoe. When we explained that we wanted to paddle ashore so that we could get to our meeting, he readily obliged. With some difficulty, we were able to get the canoe up onto the deck. We found an old board that we planned to use as a paddle. Soon, we had the canoe launched. When we both got in with our luggage, however, water began pouring in through the many cracks in the dried out canoe. We both got wet, but the launch was going so slowly that it was still within reach and we were able to climb back on board. We spread our clothes on the deck to dry in the hot sun. Though we were both amused at what had happened, I am sure that we were a forlorn-looking duo sitting there in the sun.

As I was gazing out across the sea, I could see two tiny specks in the distance. From experience, I knew that those specks were two fishermen in their tiny canoes. I suddenly got an idea. I got up on the highest portion of the launch and began calling to them, waving my white handkerchief. Eventually, I caught their attention and I signaled them to come. Soon, they were within hearing distance and I began negotiating with them to paddle us ashore. They each agreed to each take one of us for a peso each.

When I gingerly stepped into my canoe with my bag in tow, I thought the canoe would sink. It only had about an inch of buoyancy! George's canoe had only a little more!

"It's only a mile," I said and we headed for shore.

When we arrived at the shore, we gladly paid each fisherman the one peso he had requested. Soon, a bus heading for Cebu City came along and though there were no available seats, we gladly climbed into the bodega at the back. Fortunately, there were only a few pigs and chickens as our companions. Before long, we were in Cebu City and heading for the guesthouse. The relief on the faces of our family members was obvious. They had no idea why we were late or what had happened to us. They could only trust that God was, once again, taking care of us.

That trip of only one hundred twenty five miles, as the crow flies, had taken thirty-six hours! Compare this with the twenty hours it now takes to fly from Manila to the United States. The accommodations are a bit different also. I remember George asking, while gazing up into the night sky on a similar trip,

"I wonder how many times the astronauts fly completely around the world while we travel only one hundred miles?"

Through the many years that have passed, George and I have often laughed as we have recalled that trip. I also remember with amusement the advice given by one of the mission executives before we left the states for our first term of service. "When you go to the mission field," he advised, "take your sense of humor with you, and leave your sense of smell behind." It was good advice. I always felt that, though it did take grace and humor to endure some of the situations we male missionaries found ourselves in on trips like that one, it took a lot more grace for our wives and families to remain calm—not knowing what had happened to us or why we hadn't arrived at the expected time. I thank God for a calm, God-trusting wife.

"You will keep in perfect peace him whose mind is steadfast, because he trusts in you. Trust in the LORD forever, for the LORD is the Rock eternal." (Isa.26:3-4)

Twenty-Three

JUST LIKE NICODEMUS

Shortly after we moved to our new church property in Masbate City, I began showing various Christian films in our church. At that time there was a ban on showing the Martin Luther film in public places in the Philippines. I, however, felt that the government could not restrict what was shown on our privately owned property. I decided to show the film in our church. Our people invited their friends and the church was packed. When I saw the impact the film had on the people, I announced that I would show the film privately on the following night to any priests who would come. I encouraged the people to invite the priests. I wondered what would happen. I prayed that the Lord would work.

The following night as I prepared for the showing, I wondered if any priests would come. I was thrilled when one priest and two seminarians arrived accompanied by two medical doctors. After a short conversation, I started the film. Everyone listened very attentively.

After the showing there was a moment of silence. The priest then turned to me and exclaimed: "That was a wonderful film. By the way,

Becky, Paul, Elenor, Dick, Dan, Debra, Steven, 1975

could you tell me something? I've been wondering, how many different kinds of Protestants are there?"

I could see that all of his companions were very impressed with what they had seen. I knew that the priest was trying to put up a smoke screen to distract them from the impact of what they had seen.

"To tell you the truth," I answered, "I don't know. But I guess I could give you a comparison."

"To what would you compare it, then?" asked the priest.

"I think there are just about as many different kinds of Protestants as there are different kinds of Catholics."

"What do you mean? There is only one kind of Catholic!" was the quick reply of the priest.

"Really," I answered. "What about Dominicans, Franciscans, Jesuits, etc., etc.?"

"Oh, we are all the same. We are all Roman Catholics."

"If you are all the same, why is it that at one time in history all Jesuits were excommunicated from the Roman Catholic Church?" I asked.

This led to a discussion that was fast becoming a debate. I realized that the priest would make no concessions in front of the seminarians and the two medical doctors, so I suggested that we not make a debate out of it but that we each just think about what we had seen in the film. I then requested that they allow me to give them my personal testimony. When they agreed, I shared with them how that I had found the free gift of forgiveness and eternal life in Jesus Christ. I emphasized the fact that I now was absolutely sure I was going to heaven. With that, the meeting ended.

One night some weeks later, I was sitting in our living room about eight o'clock in the evening when there was a knock at the door. When I opened the door, I did not recognize the man standing in the semi-darkness until he blurted out: "I know it is late, but time doesn't make any difference between brothers, does it?"

I realized that he was the priest who had seen the Martin Luther film. I had not recognized him immediately because he was dressed in street clothes instead of his usual priestly robe. Apparently, he did not want the public to recognize him coming to my house.

"No," I answered. "Come on in."

Before he was even seated, he continued: "I have come here tonight just like Nicodemus. I don't know where I am going, and I just can't forget what you said—that a man can know. Can you tell me more?"

Before the evening was over, he asked: "Could you help me get to the United States so I can enroll in your seminary there?" I explained that there were some very important decisions that he would first have to make. I told him that the first step was to surrender in full faith to Jesus Christ. I recommended that he continue studying his Bible. I also loaned him two books written by former priests, as well as some other literature. I then prayed with him and he left. When I tried to follow him up the following days, I discovered that he had immediately been transferred out of the province.

During the first week of our stay in Masbate, Viciente Ataviado, the Vicar of Masbate, had come to our home on a friendly visit. After the treatment the priests had given us in Cebu, I was quite surprised by his visit. Since that first visit, he had returned several times. We became very friendly and sometimes we exchanged reading materials. We were often on the same platform during public functions. Sometimes he was asked to give the invocation and I the closing prayer or visa versa. Apparently, he was the one who had seen to it that the other priest was transferred out of the province.

I also suspected that he was, himself, curious about the Martin Luther film. As a result of my many conversations with him, I became convinced that he was troubled in his own soul. When Jerry Osbron came to Masbate to serve as the youth director of the Masbate Baptist Church, he began showing *Moody Science* films at the local colleges. These films always presented a strong biblical message and stressed how the Bible and science were not in conflict. Viciente even gave permission to show these films at the Liseo de Masbate, the Catholic school. He apparently watched each showing from his convent window.

One night, he asked Jerry to let him see the Martin Luther film. Of course, Jerry very willingly arranged for a private showing at the Osbron residence. It seemed to both Jerry and me that God was really working in his heart, so we sent out a special joint prayer letter to our supporters requesting prayer for his conversion. Some time later, he too, was transferred out of the province, so we were never able to confirm that he actually made the all-important decision.

I believe many Roman Catholics are convinced that many of the teachings and practices of their church are wrong. Many are now reading their Bibles. It is, however, exceedingly difficult for them to leave the Catholic Church. We need to pray that they will not only find the truth but that they will have the grace and strength to take a stand for the truth.

Twenty-Four

A PLANE GOES DOWN ON BURIAS

At about seven o'clock one evening, while we were having special meetings in the Masbate Baptist Church, I was shocked to see three white men walk into our service. One I recognized as Dr. Lincoln Nelson, a medical doctor whom I had met at the Baptist Hospital in Malaybalay, Bukidnon. He introduced his companions. One was Bob Griffin, the chief mechanic for JARRS, the aeronautical arm of theWycliff Bible translators , the other a visitor from England.

"What in the world are you doing in Masbate?" I asked.

"You mean to tell me Anderson hasn't arrived?" they asked in dismay.

"Anderson who?" I asked.

"Vernon Anderson, the missionary with the Cherokee 180."

"No," I answered, "there is no Anderson here."

"Oh my, he must not have made it!"

They then explained that they were flying from Manila with a planeload of medicine when they ran into trouble. The plane was owned by Vernon Anderson—a "Things to Come" missionary living in Tagbilaran, Bohol. Dr. Nelson, who is also a pilot, had asked Vernon to let him pilot the plane as he wanted to get in some flying hours. Vernon had agreed and climbed into the back seat. It was a very cloudy day, and since they didn't have instrumentation, they were forced to fly under the clouds in order to see where they were.

They were following the coastline of Burias when Vernon noticed gasoline dripping from the overflow of the left wing tank.

"I thought I told you to shift the fuel selector to the left tank," Vernon exclaimed.

"I did," answered Dr. Nelson.

"Well how come there is still gasoline dripping out of the overflow?"

Hearing this, Bob Griffin, an expert mechanic, immediately jumped into action. He soon discovered the fuel selector valve was not functioning. They tried to get at it but had no tools with which to pry up the floor panels where the selector was located.. After figuring the amount of time they had already been in the air, they realized that at most they had only ten minutes' worth of gasoline left in the right tank.

"Let me take her," shouted Bob, who was used to landing on short grass strips in the mountains of Mindanao.

The south west coast of Burias Island, over which they were flying, has only a few, wide sandy beaches. Much of the coastline is composed of rocky cliffs going almost directly into the ocean. By God's grace, they happened to be directly over Maputing Baybay, which is probably the only beach on that side of the island where one could possibly land a plane. It was St. John's Day (June 24)—the day most Filipinos go to the ocean for a swim in honor of John the Baptist. As they circled to come in for a landing, people scattered in all directions.

They landed safely on the beach with no apparent damage to the plane. Now able to get under the plane, they were soon able to fix the fuel selector. An expansion pin had fallen out. As they evaluated their situation, they realized that there was no way they could possibly take off again with a loaded plane. Vernon knew how much distance he needed to take off, and after stepping it out, figured he could make it with no passengers and no load if he waited for the tide to go out. A check of the tide charts revealed that the tide would go out at about five o'clock.

Fortunately, there was a rather large motorized outrigger canoe on the beach and they were able to hire it to take the three passengers and all of their cargoes to Masbate. They even took the seats out to lighten the plane as much as possible. Finishing this job, they shoved off for Masbate, hoping that Vernon would be able to take off when the tide went out and then land at the Masbate Airport and wait for them to arrive. The trip had taken six hours by boat.

After the service at the church was finished, we all went to our house for the night. The men had eaten nothing since breakfast, so Elenor fixed a hearty meal for them. After discussing the situation, we decided that there was nothing we could do until morning. After spending time in prayer for Vernon, we all went to bed.

At 2:00 a.m. I was awakened by someone knocking at our door. It was Vernon.

"I didn't make it!" he exclaimed as I opened the door.

"What happened?" I asked. By this time, the other men were also awake.

"I tried to stay as close to the water as possible because the beach was firmer there. When I got up almost enough speed to lift off, I must have gotten too close to the water and the plane swung to the right—I landed in the ocean. Fortunately there were enough people on the beach that when I called for them to help, we were able to pick the plane up and set it back on the beach.

"How much damage was done?" asked Bob.

"The right wing is damaged, the prop is bent, and the engine is full of salt water."

Vernon was thankful to be alive but was pretty downhearted about losing his precious plane. He could see no way of getting it off the island for repairs.

The next morning, I questioned Bob Griffin about various possibilities. He had helped rescue and rebuild several crashed planes.

"You'd have to have a landing barge to get that plane out," he said. "That's the only way that I can think of."

"Let me go and take a look," I said. "Sometimes there is a barge that docks at our pier."

A quick search soon revealed there was no landing barge at the pier, so I looked around to see what was available. I noticed there was a very large outrigger canoe in port with only a canvas roof. When I examined it, I saw that the roof could easily be removed.

I went back to the house to talk things over with Bob.

"Supposing we dismantle the plane and load it onto an outrigger canoe," I suggested.

"There's no outrigger canoe large enough to carry that plane," he exclaimed. "Furthermore, we don't have the special tools needed to remove the wings."

"What tools would we need?" I asked.

To his amazement, I had every tool he mentioned. I took the men down to the pier and we began negotiating with the owner of the boat. We finally convinced him to remove the roof from his boat and go to Burias for the plane.

I called Domingo Absolon, my best carpenter, and several others to help. I purchased several sheets of three-quarter inch plywood, nails, ropes, and some bamboo poles. We then went to the house, and loaded up my tools, a generator, lights, and a chain hoist. After a hearty lunch, we took off for Burias. We arrived at Maputing Baybay just as it was getting dark.

"Domingo, build a platform under the fuselage so we can lift it onto the boat when we get the wings and engine off," I instructed.

Unloading plane

I then instructed someone else to string up lights and get the generator going. Bob and I began removing the bolts that attached the engine to the fuselage. When we were ready, we called for help and loaded the engine onto the boat. Next, we began working on the wings. By about four o'clock, we had both wings tied to the outriggers of the canoe.

Just then, the wind began blowing fiercely. It was obvious that a storm was coming in. I quickly realized that our boat, which we had manipulated to a position parallel to the beach, was in grave danger. We had moved the boat to this position to make it easier to load the plane. Now, it would certainly break apart if waves pounded against it—bouncing it up and down. We had to get it off the beach!

Our problem was that we couldn't lift the fuselage. It was too heavy. I began yelling at the top of my voice for help in the local dialect in hopes that someone in the nearby village would hear me. Apparently my cry was heard, as a group of men came running.

I asked them to help lift the fuselage onto the boat. This was accomplished in only a few moments, and I yelled for everyone to shove the boat into the water. When we were out a short distance from shore, I instructed all on board to tie a rope onto anything that was heavy and throw it overboard as an anchor. The waves were big and the wind was strong, but the anchors held. In less than half an hour, the storm blew over, and soon the sun began coming up in the east. When the waves had calmed, we set out for Masbate.

When we neared the pier at Masbate, people could hardly believe their eyes! A Cherokee 180 riding on an outrigger canoe! Impossible!

I carried a plane with one hand

We tied the boat to the pier and I went to the home of Congressman Emilio Espinosa to request the use of his vacant hangar at the airport for our crippled plane. He readily agreed, so we moved our boat to a location as near as possible to the airport. Domingo Absolon lived in that area of town, so he asked his neighbors to come and help us. What a sight to see the fuselage of a plane being carried down the street on the shoulders of about ten men!

We spent the remainder of that day and part of the next trying to do everything possible to prevent the salt water from corroding and destroying the plane. I brought my air compressor to the hangar and power-sprayed everything with diesel fuel. We also filled the engine with diesel fuel.

To make a long story short, Piper, the manufacturer of the plane took partial responsibility for the accident. They had discovered that they had used a defective expansion pin in the fuel selector on that particular model. They had sent out a repair kit for all planes that they had been able to locate, but had not found this particular plane in the Philippines. They sent a new wing, propeller, carpets and all of the other parts we needed free of charge. The mechanics at Philippine Airlines overhauled the engine. Then Bob, Vernon, and I reassembled the plane, and a few months later, it was back in service.

How thankful we were for God's obvious protection and guidance in the whole affair. His ways are not our ways, but He sure knows what He is doing!

Twenty-Five

STRANGE FOOD... GREAT FUN!

In 1971, Dr. Clarence Bass of Bethel Seminary, together with his wife and daughter, visited the Philippines. Dr. Bass brought several messages at our Field Council meetings in Cebu and then traveled with us by ship to Masbate. We spent from Wednesday morning until 11:30 Thursday night together on the ship. One reason the trip took so long was that we took a detour to pass by Leyte Island to pick up some cattle to be shipped to Manila. Though it was a long trip, we enjoyed our time of fellowship, and the Bass family enjoyed watching the loading of the cattle. The cattle were forced to swim out to the ship with their heads tied to a lifeboat that was used to bring them along side the ship. The ship's derrick then lifted them by ropes tied around their horns onto the deck of the ship.

One day during the Bass visit, our boys, Paul, Dan, and Steve, informed Elenor that they wanted to prepare the meat to go with the noon meal. They had shot several large fruit bats (two to three foot wing span) with their slingshots and wanted to share the delicacy with the Bass family. After

Loading water buffalo

skinning the bats and marinating them for several hours, they roasted them over a charcoal fire.

Steve with fruit bat

When we were called to the table, no one informed the Bass family what they were eating. Dr. Bass commented on the tasty meat and wondered what it was. Our boys, without answering, encouraged him to have some more as they had prepared plenty. Only after the meal was finished did the boys excitedly explain that the delicious meat was bat. The shocked look that came over the faces of both Mrs. Bass and Carolyn brought shrieks of laughter from my boys! I explained that fruit bats eat fruit and are perfectly edible. Having grown up on the farm, I knew what pigs and chickens often eat, and I explained that perhaps bat meat is a better choice than either pork or chicken.

One morning, after the Bass family had left, we seated ourselves at the table to enjoy a pancake breakfast. I was just finishing my first pancake when our daughter Becky startled us by shrieking, "There is a lizard in the syrup!" I had noticed nothing and the syrup had tasted very good, but everyone stopped eating and jumped up from the table. Sure enough, when we looked down into the syrup pitcher there was a lizard that had gotten more than its fill of the attractive sweet substance. Before anyone was interested in finishing their breakfast, Elenor had to get out clean plates and make both new pancakes and syrup. After that incident, the kids formed a habit of always examining the pitcher carefully before using any syrup. We did, however, appreciate the lizards that were always running around the walls and ceilings of our house—they enjoyed eating bugs just as much as they did syrup!

Twenty-Six

A NEW WAY OF BUILDING CHURCHES

During December of 1971, I spent a good deal of time preparing materials and making plans for the construction of the church in Dimasalang, Masbate. Then one night, there was a fire in one of the hardware stores in Masbate City, and of course, I was one of the volunteer fire fighters. Through great effort, we were able to contain the fire to only one building—the one in which galvanized pipes and roofing were stored.

When I was convinced that the fire was out, I wearily went home and went immediately to bed. Later, I awoke with a start. In a dream I had seen the large pile of scorched galvanized water pipe that remained where the hardware supply building had been. For some time, I had been trying to think of a better way to build a strong, typhoon and termite-proof building. Seeing that pile of pipe gave me an idea. I jumped out of bed and immediately began drawing a construction design that would

Church ready for New Life Crusade in Dimasalang

use poured concrete with ribbed plywood forms and six inch spacers made of half-inch pipe, through which half-inch bolts would be placed as retainers.

The following morning, I went to the owner of the store and offered to buy the entire pile of half-inch scorched pipe. He couldn't understand why I would want to buy scorched pipe but was glad to sell the whole pile at almost a "give-away" price. I hauled the pipe home and instructed a young man who was working for me to begin cutting all of the pipes into six-inch lengths. I then hired my carpenter to help me make the forms that I had designed. I was convinced that I had discovered a way to build a poured concrete building that would be stronger, cheaper, and go up much faster than using hollow blocks.

By this time, we had a church plant in Dimasalang and had already purchased a strategically located lot for a church building. I decided to try out my new design on the Dimasalang Church. I first met with the members and encouraged them to begin carrying pails of sand from the nearby seashore to the church site in preparation for the construction. I wanted the salty beach sand to be rained on for several weeks to wash out the salt before using it in construction.

One problem we faced was that there was no good source of gravel near Dimasalang. I finally decided that the best solution was to offer to buy chipped rock and coral by the cubic foot. Many poor people began gathering chips of stone and coral along the seashore. Others began chipping away with hammers on the numerous rocks in the area. Both men and women joined in the task. Soon, sacks of aggregate were stacked all along the edge of the road. Our aggregate problem was solved.

One big advantage of poured concrete over hollow blocks is that the walls are composed of 50 percent aggregate and are thus stronger and cheaper. Another is the ease with which reinforcing rebar can be placed in the walls. With the severe typhoons and earthquakes that are so prevalent in Masbate, I wanted to make sure that any buildings we built could withstand both.

The next step in constructing the Dimasalang church was to move the needed equipment to the site. This included a gasoline-driven cement mixer, wheelbarrows, a thickness planer, and a table saw. The latter two were needed because the lumber to be used in the construction of the roof structure of the church and the framing of the parsonage came directly to Dimasalang from Leyte Island by outrigger canoe. This lumber was hand-sawed and quite rough.

I preferred it, however, to the sawmill lumber coming from Mindanao. The lumber from Leyte was much harder and stronger because Leyte is in the center of the typhoon belt, and trees on Leyte are continually beaten by strong winds. Mindanao seldom experiences either a strong typhoon or strong winds so the lumber from there is much softer.

Since no one in the Philippines had seen the type of construction I was planning, I found it necessary to work with the construction crew. During the first days, it was often raining and the construction site became very muddy, so I sometimes went barefoot just like the rest of the crew. At times, we sank up to our ankles in the mud. The work went smoothly, however, and the building rapidly took shape. People were amazed to observe both the speed of the work and the type of construction. They had never seen a building constructed without first pouring the posts and the superstructure. They could not see how a building could be strong without posts.

As they watched, they soon became convinced that this type of construction was indeed very strong. At the end of five weeks, both the church and the parsonage were ready for use. We had even constructed about twenty pews during that time. As planned, we did not finish the wall facing the street so that we could have temporary seating all the way to the street, if needed. This temporary seating was made from the coconut trees we had cut down right there on the church site.

In leveling the lot, we had actually cut into a hill at the back of the lot. This had left an eighteen-foot cliff right behind the church. One day, when I had to leave the site for a few hours, I instructed the crew to cut down a coconut tree that was located right at the edge of this cliff, directly behind the church. I was afraid that someday it might be blown down and topple onto the church. I left a long rope for them to tie to the tree and showed them how to cut it in such a way that it would fall up hill and not onto the church.

When I returned, I was shocked to see that they had not followed my instructions and the tree had fallen right onto a fifteen-foot high wall that we had just poured the day before. I was disgusted with them for not following my instructions but proud that the tree, and not the wall, had broken in two. People were now really becoming convinced of the strength of this type of construction.

After the building was complete, we began a "New Life Crusade" in the new building. The team was composed of Pastor and Mrs. Sabido, Rev. Cris Batuto, and me. The local members also assisted in many ways. Rev. Batuto, the excellent chalk artist and evangelist, did a good job. Each night, we first showed one of the filmstrips we had prepared with recorded Masbatiño soundtracks. Special music and a chalk-illustrated message by Rev. Batuto followed this. We continued for five weeks and 300-500 people attended each night.

Batuto – chalk artist – evangelist

During the first two weeks, we used mostly Old Testament filmstrips to lay a foundation for the presentation of the gospel. After laying a good foundation for the gospel message, we began giving an invitation to surrender to Jesus Christ and accept Him as Lord and Savior. Each night, many responded.

During the crusade, Cris Batuto and I stayed in the newly constructed parsonage. Incidentally, the floors and some of the walls of the parsonage were made from the plywood that had been used as forms in the construction of the church. Mrs. Caspi from Cataingan cooked for us. I stayed healthy the whole time and learned to eat fish and rice three times a day. It was very hot during the crusade and I was glad there was enough water in the well we had dug so that I could bathe at least three times a day.

During the last weeks of the crusade, Pastor Nilo Veloso and his family arrived in Masbate to begin language study and to make preparations for their move to Ticao Island. We had asked them to help us start a new work on Ticao. We had long been concerned about evangelizing that island and had received many letters from listeners to our daily radio program "The Voice of Truth" who lived there. The Velosos are a very musical family and were able to help with special music during the last days of the crusade. Being present for part of the crusade enabled them to observe how we conducted the crusade and this proved to be good training for them in preparation for a crusade we would later hold in Ticao.

One night during the Dimasalang crusade, Clair Layman and Charlie Barrows, the father of Cliff Barrows of the Billy Graham Association, came to observe the crusade and also to see the new church building. They were in Masbate at my request to distribute Gideon New Testaments and Bibles in all of the schools and to all government officials.

I took time off from the Dimasalang crusade to escort Charlie and Clair in their distribution work. Shortly after the distribution in Masbate, Monsignor Lachica, the parish priest in the town of Mobo, ordered that the Bibles that had been distributed in Mobo be collected and publicly burned. Many Catholic priests were teaching at that time that it was a sin for a layman to read the Bible. To my knowledge, it was only Monsignor Lachica who went to the point of ordering the actual burning of Bibles.

The results of the crusade in Dimasalang were very encouraging. As I had expected, a higher percentage of those who made professions continued on and joined the church than in previous crusades held in our large "gospel tents." The fact that we already had a beautiful church building on a permanent location eliminated the loss that had previously taken place in moving from a tent to a second location. The fact that Pastor Sabido was already on location as pastor and was known by the people was also important.

Pastor Sabido led the program each night, and we did our best to build him up in the eyes of the people all during the crusade. During the latter part of the crusade, when we started special Bible studies for the new converts, we insisted that he lead them. We wanted people to look to him for leadership, as he was the one who would be staying in Dimasalang.

Mobo Baptist Church

This method of church planting and church construction proved to be very successful. We no longer use tent crusades. Most churches start as Bible studies conducted by members of neighboring churches or by Bible School graduates who are sent to a specific area to start a new work. When a pastor is already on the field and a group of believers are organized, we then try to

129

buy a lot in a good location and construct a permanent church building in which to conduct a town or citywide crusade. The type of construction first tested in Dimasalang is usually used. It has turned out to be much cheaper and much stronger than using hollow blocks. Since the Dimasalang crusade, many churches have been constructed using variations of the Dimasalang Church. Mobo Baptist Church (pictured) is one of them.

Twenty-Seven

A MIRACULOUS DREAM

One day, as I was sitting at the front desk of our Ikthus Youth Center which we had opened on the lower floor of the Masbate Baptist Church, a very attractive well-dressed lady in her early thirties walked in. She had a puzzled look on her face and exclaimed, "Here I am. What do you want?"

I returned her puzzled look and asked what she was talking about. She looked me straight in the eye and said, "He told me to come to the Baptist Church. Here I am."

"Who is he? What are you talking about?" I asked.

"My name is Vilma Reyes," she explained. "I am a teacher in the Masbate Comprehensive High School. When I came home from school this afternoon, I was very tired so I lay down on our couch and fell asleep. In my sleep, I dreamed that my husband and I were lost in the middle of a desert. We were dying of thirst and dehydration. As we struggled on, I looked up and saw in the distance a little house about the size of an outhouse. I thought I must be seeing a mirage, but my husband saw it too. We began running towards it, hoping we would find water or help of some kind. When we reached it, we found that sand had drifted against the door. We dug frantically with our hands until we finally got it open. When we stepped inside we were disappointed—the building appeared to be empty."

"When we looked down, however, we saw something sticking up out of the sand! It looked like the handle of something. When we brushed away the sand, we discovered that it was the handle of a wooden chest. We thought it must be a treasure chest! We dug frantically with our hands until we got it out. Fortunately, we were able to pry it open. To our surprise, it was filled with black books marked 'Holy Bible.' As we began to examine them, a voice from somewhere very clearly said 'Go to the Baptist Church.' Just then I woke up. As I pondered my dream, I decided to obey the instruction. Here I am. What do you want?"

By this time, I had had enough experience to know that God does sometimes speak through dreams—especially in areas of the world where the word of God is not well known. I immediately assumed that God had spoken to her and I told her so. I got out my "Holy Bible" and explained that the Bible is God's book and that it contains a special message for her. I explained that her situation was very similar to that of which she had dreamed. I explained that all people have a great thirst deep down in their hearts that can only be quenched when we drink from the living water—Jesus Christ.

Jerry Osbron in front of Ikthus

As I showed her verse after verse, it was obvious that the Holy Spirit was working in her heart. When I got to the point of explaining the importance of her repenting of her sins and asking Jesus Christ to forgive her, she nodded her head in agreement. I explained her need to surrender to Jesus Christ as her Lord and trust Him as her Savior.

"Would you like to do this right now?" I asked.

She looked up with tears streaming down her face and said, "Yes I would."

As we both bowed our heads, she prayed a simple but beautiful prayer of repentance and surrender to Jesus Christ. When she had finished praying, it was obvious that peace and joy had flooded her soul. Her thirst had been quenched!

Vilma grew rapidly in her Christian faith and witness. Soon, several members of her family, including her husband, also accepted the Lord. She and her husband later shared with me how she had previously scolded him when she caught him listening to our daily radio program, "The Voice of Truth." Being a devout Roman Catholic, she did not want him influenced by the teachings of those "heretical Protestants." She did admit, however, that for sometime the Holy Spirit had been speaking to her through the witness of some of her co-teachers who were members of the Masbate Baptist Church. How wonderfully God intervened with a dream to draw her to Himself!

Vilma soon became a very bold witness for Jesus Christ. Sometimes I was afraid that she might lose her job as a public school teacher because of it. Not only did she boldly witness in the classroom, she sometimes brought her whole class to the church and asked one of our pastors to conduct a Bible class for them. When I warned her that she might be endangering her position as a public school teacher, she looked at me as though shocked that I would even consider such an eventuality as a reason to stop persuading people to accept Jesus Christ.

Twenty-Eight

LIFE ASSURANCE

All conversions are amazing, but several stand out in my mind. One was the conversion of Mr. Tusing, a pioneer of the Philippine Life Insurance Company for the province of Masbate. He was the president of the Holy Name Society in the Catholic Church. He had even received a papal citation for his outstanding work in the Catholic Church. He came to my house one day to collect payment for the fire insurance on our house. During our conversation, he proposed that I buy a life insurance policy. I told him I was very interested if he had the right kind of policy.

"What kind of a policy are you looking for?" he asked.

"I want a policy that states that when I die, I am the beneficiary."

"We don't have a policy like that!" he exclaimed with a strange expression on his face.

"Well, if you don't, let me explain for you a policy we have that has that benefit." He was amazed as I explained to him God's policy of "life assurance." Some of the Bible verses I used he had never read before, and he expressed doubt that they were in a Catholic Bible.

Papal citation awarded to Vicente Tusing

"Do you have a Bible?" I asked.

"Yes. I have a Bible that was given to me by the Bishop."

"Why don't we go and see if these verses are in your Bible?" I suggested.

"Let's go," he said, and soon we were reading the same verses from his Bible.

"How come the priests are hiding these truths from us?" he questioned.

One portion of Scripture that particularly influenced Mr. Tusing's rejection of the Catholic Church and her teachings was Exodus 20. In emphasizing the sinfulness of man, I often use the Ten Commandments as recorded in Exodus 20 to point out God's standard of righteousness. When we read the second commandment, Mr. Tusing was shocked.

In the Catechism used in the Philippines, the second commandment that prohibits making, bowing down to, and worshiping idols is left out. The tenth commandment is then divided into two commandments, so they still come out with Ten Commandments. This makes two commandments that deal with adultery.

Mr. Tusing began studying his Bible with great diligence, and, by God's grace, he soon surrendered to Jesus Christ as his Lord and Savior. Before long, he became a very faithful leader in our church. He was known and highly respected throughout the province. When he was later elected as a deacon of the Masbate Baptist Church, the insights he had learned in business greatly helped in the expansion of our work. He often emphasized the importance of maintaining a good public image and always being prompt at all appointments.

I believe that his conversion was the result of a special emphasis we had in the Masbate Church of praying specifically that God would give us key male leadership . Mr. Tusing and many other prominent male leaders were converted during that time, and they later gave excellent leadership to the "mother church" and to the planting of over one hundred daughter, granddaughter, and great granddaughter churches during our ministry.

Twenty-Nine

THE APOSTLE TO BURIAS

We began "The Voice of Truth," our daily radio program, on January 1, 1970. There were only two local radio stations so we aired our program twice a day on both local radio stations at the same time—6:30 a.m. and 6:30 p.m. That way, if people didn't like to listen to us on one station, they could turn to the other and listen to us there. We were on the air for twenty years and were the longest running program on a local radio station when we discontinued the program.

"The Voice of Truth" produced hundreds of amazing conversions and led to the establishment of many churches. One of the most significant conversions was Mardonio Marianito. Mardonio was a farmer living in Canumay on Burias Island. After listening to the "Voice of Truth" for some time, he one day exclaimed to his wife: "That does sound like the truth. I'm going to Masbate to find out more!"

"No you're not! You're not getting involved with any Protestants!"

Recording studio

When Mardonio insisted that he was going, his wife in anger exclaimed, "I won't give you any money for your fare!" In the Philippines, the wife often controls the pocketbook.

"Well, I'm going whether you give me any money or not!"

With that, Mardonio went down to the seashore and flagged down a passing boat. When he climbed aboard, he informed the operator of the boat that he had no money but would be glad to help with the operation of the boat if only they would allow him to ride to Masbate. Fortunately, the operator did not force him to get off.

When he arrived at the pier in Masbate, he began walking up and down the streets trying to find the Masbate Baptist Church. If he had only five cents he could have ridden on a motorized tricycle and simply instructed the driver to take him to the MBC. All drivers knew where it was. Since he had no money, he just walked until he found the church. I was out of town when he arrived, so Pastor Ed Martinez was the one to entertain him.

Mardonio with wife,
daughter-in-law
and three sons

That evening when I arrived back in Masbate, Pastor Martinez introduced Mardonio to me. "Here is a radio listener form Burias who has just accepted the Lord," Ed exclaimed. As I began conversing with Mardonio, I saw that he had leadership ability

Marianitos'
commissioning service

and was very sincere in his decision to follow the Lord. I also realized that he lived in an area of Burias where there were no evangelical churches. It was obvious that he was very intelligent and could read well, so I gave him a Bible in the Cebuano dialect, which he understood. I encouraged him to continue listening to "the Voice of Truth" and to read his Bible daily. I also encouraged him to put into practice everything he learned from the Bible and to teach it to his family and neighbors. I prayed with and for him and we said goodbye.

Little did I realize at that time the significance of that conversion and the way he would open our eyes to see that "lay people" can be greatly used in spreading the gospel and establishing new churches. Mardonio continued to grow in his spiritual life, and on October 7, 1975, he followed the Lord in baptism. After his baptism, we encouraged him to begin holding worship services in his home and to invite his friends and relatives to attend.

After only a few months, we received a letter from Mardonio requesting us to come and baptize his converts. When I first read his letter, I wondered what this could mean. I wondered what kind of converts he would have and if they would really be ready for baptism. When I consulted with the church board, they unanimously felt that we should go and investigate.

So it was that several of the deacons and I headed for Burias in the motorized outrigger canoe that belonged to one of our members. When we arrived in Canumay, Mardonio immediately began introducing us to his converts. These converts included his wife and children, as well as several neighbors and friends. It was obvious that they were very sincere people, so I encour-

Early converts in Conumay

aged the deacons to begin interviewing them to ascertain if they were ready for baptism. While this was going on, I had a sharing time with Mardonio. When the interviews were complete, the deacons came to me with shining faces, exclaiming that they had never interviewed people so well prepared for baptism!

"Wonderful!" I answered. "Then let's have a baptism!"

After a beautiful public baptismal service along the seashore, we went back to Mardonio's house for something to eat. As we sat around the table, we began making plans for the future of the work in Canumay.

"We need a pastor assigned to Canumay," exclaimed Mardonio.

"I agree with you," I answered.

"Who will it be?" asked Mardonio.

"The pastor will be you," I answered.

My statement shocked Mardonio. Perhaps the others attending were also shocked. I was slowly getting my eyes opened to the fact that the qualifications for being a bishop (pastor) according to the New Testament had much more to do with character and spiritual gifts than they did with formal education. After I explained why I thought Mardonio was the man for the job, everyone present seemed to agree with me—every one, that is, except Mardonio himself. He was very hesitant.

We did our best to convince him that God would be with him and give him everything he needed to do the job. We promised to pray for him and to do what we could to help him. We placed our hands on Mardonio and prayed over him, committing him to the service of the Lord. After we said goodbye, we headed back to Masbate. The story of the years that followed and the planting of many churches on the Island of Burias and surrounding areas reads like the Book of Acts.

In June of 1978, just two days before we were to leave on our fourth furlough, I received a letter from David Pepito—a radio listener. The letter stated that he lived in Malubago, Burias and had been listening to our radio broadcast and wanted to start a church in his barrio. He asked that I come and visit him. I had been to Burias many times, but I had no idea where Malubago was. I took the letter to Pastor Martinez and asked if he knew. He also had never heard of the place. When I asked him if he would try to find out and then follow up this request, he stated that, with all of the responsibilities of Acting Senior Pastor now his, there was no way that he would have time to go to Burias.

I didn't know what to do. The letter sounded very sincere, and David had said that many of his neighbors were also interested. Then I thought of Mardonio Marianito. I quickly wrote a letter asking him to come immediately to Masbate, as I needed to see him before leaving for the states. I then took the letter to the pier to see if any boat had arrived from the north side of Burias. Fortunately, there was one, so I asked the owner of the boat if he would deliver the letter to Mardonio. I impressed upon him the urgency of getting the letter to Mardonio as soon as possible. He agreed to do his best.

The following day, Mardonio arrived in Masbate. I showed him Pepito's letter and asked him if he knew where Malubago was located.

"Sure, I know where it is. It's north of us about eight hours by paddle boat."

"Would you be willing to follow up this contact?" I asked, "Would you be willing to paddle up there?"

"Sure, I'd be glad to," was his immediate response. "What do you want me to do?"

"Do exactly the same thing there that you have been doing in Canumay. Lead people to the Lord and help them to organize a church."

Mardonio took the challenge, and I placed my hands on him and committed him to the Lord. I prayed for his success. When I looked up, both of us had tears in our eyes. I didn't know what would happen, but somehow I felt that God's hand was leading. The following day, we left Masbate, headed for Manila and then on to the states.

During our furlough, we received one letter from Mardonio from which I will quote a portion.

About the task that you've assign me in Malubago, I am very thankful that they very faithful in following Jesus Christ. They are the fastly growing in Christ. Last September 16, 1978, Pastor Martinez baptized 16 souls. And from that time there ten souls receives Christ and they ready for baptismal class. Now I open 5 barrios for Bible studies. These places needs a fulltime worker. They needs to visit twice a week. Now I have to divided my time I have to reach two to three barrios weekly and to stay there for 2 to 3 days. Now I have to meet many problems – especially my daily needs. We are suffering more but this suffering cannot get away my belief in Jesus Christ for I know there will be a time that God gives His blessing to me. During the visit of Miss Dimatera & Mrs. Balona in Canumay they have witness how we suffer.

The following barrios that I'm serving for Bible studies are:

1. Sitio Malapinggan (Navasagan) -11 received Christ as personal Lord and Savior.

2. Sitio Mattayattay – 12 souls receive Christ as personals Lord and Savior.

3. Pasig, Bodega, Ki-putol.

These places I have to hike with my wife about 20 kilometers. These barrios need a full-time worker to follow up. And I hope that you can suggest what more can I do. So I want to hear a news from you.

I answered his letter and encouraged him to carry on as best he could. I pointed out that suffering is part of the Christian life and that Jesus had warned that all who followed Him would experience it. I told him that though I had personally experienced little suffering we should consider suffering for Christ a privilege.

One day, soon after we arrived back in Masbate, Mardonio came to Masbate for some fellowship and to see me. As I observed him, I noticed that something seemed to be wrong. When I asked how he was getting along, he gave his usual response "Just fine." When I questioned him further, he admitted that he had just had a problem with his wife.

"What happened?" I asked.

"Well, I recently made a trip to Malubago. When I left that morning, I forgot about the water buffalo and left it tied in the sun. When my wife found it, it was almost dead. (*A water buffalo has no sweat glands and if left in the sun, needs to be cooled off by submerging itself in a water hole or by having water poured over it.*) When I got home, she was very angry. She accused me of neglecting my family—'always running off preaching the gospel. Look at our corn! You've neglected our farm! What are we going to eat?'"

"What did you do?" I asked.

"Since what she was saying was true, I decided to call a family meeting to discuss the issue."

"What did you decide?" I asked.

"Well, after discussing the issue for some time, we decided to sell the water buffalo before it dies. I can still farm using just a bolo knife but I cannot stop preaching the gospel. There is no one else to spread the message."

Oh, for more people with that kind of commitment! When the rewards are passed out in heaven, there will be many unsung heroes who will be honored with greater honors than many of us who receive honors down here!

September 2, 1979, was a day to remember in the Masbate Baptist Church. It was on that day that the church officially commissioned Mr. and Mrs. Mardonio Marianito as our missionaries to Burias Island. The church had been observing the success of their volunteer missionary work and decided that it was high time to give them both the recognition and support they deserved. The church agreed to support them with a monthly allowance and the Dalanon family, a more well-to-do family in the church, donated a boat and motor to make the Marianitos' missionary journeys a little easier.

Shortly after that, Pastor Martinez and I rode with Mardonio in his boat to Malubago to see the new work there and to baptize the converts. When we got there, it was a thrill to see that they had already built a very presentable chapel made of native materials with a galvanized iron roof. By the time the service began, there were about forty in attendance, and of these we baptized seven that day. We spent some time in Malubago instructing the new believers and also visiting an outreach they had already established in the barrio of Kintina. What a joy to observe how God used the Marianito family to further his kingdom. It was also thrilling to see how others are following their footsteps and sacrificing in many ways to spread the gospel. As we fellowshipped with them, ate their food, and slept with them on their floors each night, the stories they told sounded much like the book of Acts.

Mardonio continued to reach new areas. He helped plant a church in Claveria—one of the two county seats on the Island of Burias. For several years, he served as its pastor. Then on May 10, 1995, a wonderful ordination service was

Early baptism in
Malubago, Burias

held in the Claveria Baptist Church. By this time, Mardonio's son, Ronel, had graduated from the Masbate Baptist Bible College and was serving as the pastor of the Claveria Church. This church observed the work of Mardonio Marianito for many years and believed that he should be officially ordained as a minister of Jesus Christ. In fact, most of those who called for the ordination were converts of Mardonio. Though he had never formally attended any Bible School or Seminary, it was obvious that he was chosen and gifted by God for the ministry. I had done my best to disciple and mentor him when he came to Masbate. The number of pastors and key leaders of the district who attended the occasion evidenced the respect everyone had for him.

Mardonio did an excellent job of presenting and defending his doctrinal statement, and the vote of the counsel to recommend his ordination by the local church was unanimous. This made him the second worker in the Masbate Southern Luzon District to be ordained who had never gone to a Bible School or Seminary. The first was Edmondo Martinez.

Thirty

OBEYING GOD'S CALL
BRINGS HAPPINESS

Flor Dimatera had been our next-door neighbor when we lived on Rosero Street in Masbate City. Her father was the retired Provincial Treasurer, and several of her family members held prominent positions in the province and in the city. Flor had struggled with the truths of the Bible for years, and we tried hard to win her for Christ. When she finally did surrender, she was the acting head of Red Cross for the province. She began growing very rapidly in her Christian life and soon became a bold and effective witness for Christ. When she gave her testimony, she often used the words of "Wasted Years," a popular Christian song at that time, to describe her previous life.

One day, she remarked about how busy the Masbate Baptist Church staff was and asked if she could help in any way. When I learned that she was an excellent typist, I invited her to help with office work. Soon, she was spending several hours almost every afternoon typing out Bible lessons and doing other types of office work. She was always very pleasant and often commented on how much she enjoyed her time in the office.

One day, after hearing this comment several times, I asked her, "Are you trying to tell me something? Are you trying to tell me that you want to work in the office full-time?"

She looked down with an embarrassed look on her face. Apparently, she didn't want to give the impression that she was looking for work. She already had an excellent well-paying job.

"I just love the work here in the office and there is so much more that needs to be done."

"Maybe God is giving you a vision of what He wants you to do with your life," I suggested.

As weeks went by, I heard her make other comments that seemed to indicate her desire to spend more time in the office. I began praying for God's clear leading in the matter. How wonderful it would be to have a full-time secretary like her! But how could we ever expect her to leave her secure position as acting head of the Red Cross to work for the church? I knew that all of the staff members of the church were receiving only a fraction of the salary she was receiving. I was also convinced that anyone who worked in the church office should be supported by the church and not by me. In addition to this, I also believed that a church secretary should receive a smaller salary than the pastor.

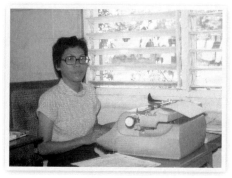

Flor Ordiz

One day, I decided to share this whole situation with the church board. They were all very much in agreement that Flor would be a wonderful addition to our church staff. They were also in agreement that she would never leave her position in the Red Cross to work for the church.

"We could never afford to pay a salary similar to what she is receiving and we could not expect her to take a cut in pay. Furthermore, her parents would never allow her to work with the Baptist Church!" explained Mr. Tusing emphatically.

"But, do you all agree that the church needs her and that she would make a wonderful addition to our staff?" I asked.

All quickly agreed.

"Then why don't we try to figure out how much the church could afford to pay and then leave the decision up to Flor?" I suggested.

Under some pressure from me, the board reluctantly agreed to make a study of the budget. They were reluctant because they all felt it was a waste of time. They felt sure that no one, including Flor, would ever leave the directorship of Red Cross to become a poorly paid secretary of a Baptist church.

A proposal was drawn up and a call issued to Flor. To the amazement of the whole church, she gladly accepted the offer and was soon working full time for the church. Through the years that followed, Flor, with her brilliant mind, excellent skills, and happy disposition, has fulfilled a vital role in God's great plan for the expansion of His work in the Province of Masbate and the whole Philippines.

When Flor resigned from the Red Cross, an official from the Red Cross tried to convince Flor to return several times. They offered her three times the salary that she was receiving from the church, but Flor could not be distracted.

"God called me to work in the church and in church work I shall remain. I have never been this happy in any position I have ever held! I shall stay where I am."

Flor's decision had a great impact on our church and on all who knew her. Many saw in her an example they should follow. Soon, Flor was not only typing our Bible study lessons—she was writing them. She developed great teaching skills, and the fact that she could never be accused of doing it for financial gain made her teaching even more effective. When we opened the Masbate Bible College, she became the registrar of the school, as well as a very effective teacher and counselor.

Thirty-One

GRAVEN IMAGES...
DEMONIC POWERS

As I evaluated the membership of our churches, I noticed that most of them lacked male leadership. This was also true of the Masbate Baptist Church. I, therefore, began to pray that God would bring many key men into his church. To my amazement, four men, who would later become leaders in the church, were converted the same night at an open-air meeting we conducted.

One of these men was Ramon Burgos. His father was of Spanish decent, so Ramon had very light skin. As we were often seen together, people began calling him the "little American." Soon, several members of his immediate family also accepted the Lord.

One day, when he heard that I was going to Manila, he asked if I would visit his sister, Mrs. Valencia, who lived in Manila while her fourteen children attended college there. She was the wife of our family physician in Masbate and a very strong Roman Catholic. She became very angry with Ramon when he converted and was baptized into our church.

She had been going through great stress as a result of a strange happening in their house.

Ramon and friend

According to her, at certain times of the night, the heavy back door of their house would rattle violently to the point that even the heavy metal hinges had been bent. She had called the Catholic Bishop and he had sprinkled holy water on the door and performed various ceremonies, but all to no avail. She had even had a Spiritista minister come and do his incantations. To her dismay, the shaking continued. She was becoming a nervous wreck and desperately needed help. Ramon wanted me to visit her because he thought that, perhaps, what was happening to her might be softening her heart to accept Jesus Christ.

When I knocked on her door, she seemed hesitant to let me in, but when I explained that her brother had sent me to help her with her problems, she invited me in. After some small talk, I asked her about what was happening in her home. I noticed that the house was filled with images of various "saints." She explained about the door and showed me the bent hinges. After examining the door, I assured her that I was certain that I could help her with her problem. I assured her that if she was willing to follow the instructions of the Bible, I would pray and God would not allow any person or spirit to rattle her door again.

"Okay," she said. "What must I do?"

"You must remove from this house everything that is in violation of God's commandments."

"There is nothing in this house that violates God's commandment," was her quick response.

"Do you have a Bible?" I asked.

She did and I suggested that we study her Bible. I opened it to Exodus 20—the Ten Commandments. She was puzzled as we read the second commandment, which forbids the making, bowing down to, or worshiping of graven images. As I pointed out in previous chapters, the second commandment is omitted in the Catholic Catechism. The tenth commandment is then divided into two parts so that there are still ten commandments. The ninth commandment in the catechism is: "Thou shall not covet your neighbor's wife," and the tenth is: "You shall not covet anything that is your neighbor's." The result of this numbering change makes the ninth commandment basically a repetition of the seventh commandment, which forbids adultery.

"What do you want me to do?" she asked.

"Obey the word of God," I answered. "You must remove everything in this house that is contrary to the word of God. I will then pray and God will protect you."

In the process of studying her Bible, I also pointed out how she could be forgiven of her sins and receive true peace with God and eternal life. She loved her images, however, and, in the end, refused to remove them. I, therefore, did not pray that God would stop whoever or whatever it was that was shaking her door. I only prayed that God would enlighten her mind and soften her heart to believe and obey His word.

After incidents such as this, I sometimes wondered if I did the right thing. I wondered if I should have first asked God to stop the shaking of the door to prove His power over all things. Perhaps then she would have believed and accepted Jesus Christ. I asked several people who specialize in dealing with evil spirits for their opinions, however, and they confirmed that I did the right thing.

Thirty-Two

I'LL SEE YOU IN THE MORNING

I received word in September 1980 that my mother's cancer had returned and that it was now considered terminal. In October, I received a telegram from my brother, Dale, stating that if I wanted to see my mother alive, I should come immediately.

After thinking over the situation, I decided I should take the first possible flight out. I had two goals for the trip. First, I wanted to spend some time with my mother while she was still alive. I thought it was more important to visit her while she was alive than to attend her funeral. Secondly, I thought that since she was in the hospital in Forest City, I would have an opportunity to share with some of my friends in Forest City the plans of the Masbate Baptist Church to build a new sanctuary. I felt certain that some of them would help financially.

However, getting from Masbate to Manila proved to be quite difficult. When the flight to Manila was cancelled, I took the launch to Bulan, Sorsogon, and then took a jeepney to Legaspi, hoping to catch a flight from there. Then when the flight from Legaspi was also cancelled, I was forced to take the overnight bus to Manila.

When I got to Manila, I was able to purchase a ticket to St. Paul, but after taking off, we were forced to return to Manila because of a bomb scare. This caused a twelve-hour delay, but I finally got to St. Paul, Minnesota at 2:30 p.m. on October 8, 1980.

I stayed with my brother Dale that night and was able to see our sons, Paul and Dan, who were studying at Bethel College. The next morning, I borrowed a car and drove to Forest City. When I walked into my mother's room at the hospital, she looked up with a smile and said, "Dick, take me home."

After a short visit with her, I went to consult her doctor who turned out to be a Filipino. I told him of my mother's request and asked his opinion. "Take her any place she wants to go," he said. "We have done everything we can for her."

When Pastor Herb Hage from the First Baptist Church heard that I was in town, he called the hospital and had me paged. He requested that I stop by the parsonage before I left Forest City. I readily agreed and stopped by his house later that afternoon.

Herb welcomed me at the door and immediately began sharing what was happening at First Baptist. "Next Sunday is a very important day in our Church!" he exclaimed. "We are going to vote on whether to relocate and build a new church building, or stay where we are. The reason I asked you to come is that I want you to pray that God will guide in this big decision."

I readily agreed to pray with them, but in my heart I was troubled. How could I share, as I had planned, with the members of the church the needs in Masbate when they were facing a big decision regarding their own church? I decided not to even mention our needs in Masbate.

That night, I slept in my mother's house in Fertile and prepared to bring Mother home the following day. Mother was still able to walk but was very thin. When we arrived at the house and I got her seated in her La-Z-Boy chair by the window, she gave a sigh of relief. It was obvious that she was glad to be home.

The next three weeks were a sad but wonderful time for both of us. I had the privilege of preparing meals for mother, as well as caring for her in every other way. We reminisced of days gone by, and she wanted to know all about the work in Masbate. She especially asked about Ticao Island, as she had been praying for that island for years. Each morning, we had our devotions.

One morning, she looked up and asked: "What is the shadow of death?" She was reading the Twenty-Third Psalm.

I always hesitated to give Mother my opinion on such things, as I felt that she knew her Bible just as well as I did.

"I'm not sure. What do you think it means?" I asked.

"Well, I'm not sure either, but I know this, you can't have a shadow without a light."

"That's good enough for me." I answered.

Mother had no hesitation in talking about death. She longed for the Lord to "take her home." When we prayed together, she would sometimes pray: "God, what are you waiting for? You know this body is shot, and I know you have a new one waiting for me." It was wonderful to observe her complete confidence in God—though she sometimes thought He was moving too slowly.

While spending time with Mother, I kept thinking about Masbate. My plan of getting assistance from our friends in Forest City had fallen through, and I wondered what I should do.

I then thought of my cousin Ivene Nelson and her husband, Les. Les was a wealthy contractor living in Clear Lake. They had already helped finance several projects for us and, I wondered if they would help again.

I decided to call and ask if I could come for a visit. "Sure. Come on down. I'd like to talk with you," was the quick response from Les.

When I arrived at their door, Les greeted me and ushered me into his office. "I've got something I want to show you. You know that I donated a lot as a site for our new church (Free Church) here in Clear Lake. Well, we've already outgrown it! We're planning an addition and I would like to have you look over the plans and make any suggestions you may have." Once again, I didn't feel that I should bring up our needs in Masbate.

After spending three weeks with my mother, I faced a problem of what to do. Mother was getting thinner and thinner, and she was having difficulty keeping her food down. Though she could pass away

My parents

at any time, I personally did not feel her death was imminent , and I felt I needed to get back to Masbate.

˙ I called my brother, Dale, to inform him that I would have to leave soon. He and his wife, Phrel, came down to Fertile to help make plans regarding Mother. After talking things over, I told Dale that I felt I should leave that day so I would have a couple of days with two sons in St. Paul before leaving for the Philippines. When it was time for me to say goodbye to Mother, Dale stepped outside—apparently not wanting to see her reaction.

It took a while but when I finally got up enough courage to tell her, I walked up to her and said, "Mom, I'm afraid I have to leave now and go back to the Philippines."

"Of course you do," she answered. "Get back there where the Lord told you to be. Don't worry about me. I'll see you in the morning!"

"Okay," I said. "You go on ahead. Greet Dad and Grandma and Grandpa from me. Tell them I'll be coming soon."

With that, I slowly turned and walked out the door. Up to that point, I had been able to keep my composure, but when I got in the car and headed for the Twin Cities, the tears began to flow. How I would miss Mother! How I would miss her newsy letters and encouragement! How I would miss her prayers!

It was Saturday, and when I arrived in St. Paul, I went immediately to find Paul and Dan so I could spend the evening with them. As the evening wore on, I asked where they were going to church the following morning. Since they had no preference, I suggested that we go to Grace Church Edina.

When we arrived at the church, we were surprised to discover that the service had already begun and an usher informed us that there were no empty seats. Just then, another usher came up to inform us that there were still three empty seats in the front row if we wanted them. We did, and as we walked down the isle and were seated, the pastor, Bob Ricker, noticed us and looked at me as if to say, "What in the world are you doing here?"

When he had finished his message, he asked me to come up on the platform and give the closing prayer. When I had finished, he immediately asked if we had gotten the money we needed for our new church building.

"Not yet," I answered.

"Then go and see Kenny," he instructed. "We just ran over our faith promise goal!"

Kenneth Kenerud was the Missions Pastor of the church, so I immediately went to find him. Kenny suggested that we meet for breakfast at a restaurant in St. Paul the following morning. When I arrived at the restaurant, Kenny got right to the point.

"I think that every mission organization has heard that we ran over our goal," he stated. "Everyone wants our help. Why should you be the one we help?"

With that, I began explaining the amazing things that were taking place in Masbate. When I had finished, Ken looked me in the eye and said, "I'll recommend that we give $35,000 towards your new building. Please remember, however, that we don't have the money. God does and we have made faith promises. Help us pray for the money."

I left the restaurant walking on air and marveling at God's timing and God's provision.

"You did not choose me, but I chose you and appointed you to go and bear fruit—fruit that will last. Then the Father will give you whatever you ask in my name." (John 15:16)

Thirty-Three

A CATHEDRAL GOES
UP IN MASBATE

When I got back to Masbate, I informed the Masbate Baptist Church of the marvelous way God had led and of the promise of the Grace Church Edina to give $35,000. This promise, together with the previous commitment of Dr. Luther, pastor of the College Avenue Baptist Church in San Diego, who said he would encourage his church give $25,000 towards our project, encouraged us to immediately elect a building committee and begin making definite plans for our new building. We remembered the advice of Dr. Luther: "Think big." We were so thankful for the wonderful way God had led in the purchase of a very choice lot adjoining our existing church property on which to build this new sanctuary.

The actual construction of our new "Cathedral," as many of the local people began calling it, took almost one year. The measurements of the building were seventy-five by one hundred and eight feet. We ran all of the structural figures through a computer at the University of the Philippines to get the proper specifications. We programmed the building to withstand the strongest recorded typhoon and the strongest recorded earthquake at the same time. I knew that, very often, people run for safety to churches during typhoons, and I wanted to make sure that our building could withstand all of the stresses and strains that would be placed upon it.

The tapered steel trusses weighed three tons each. We made them ourselves and used over 1,000 pounds of welding rods. We had two men welding from 7:00 a.m. to 5:00 p.m. almost every day for three months. I had never constructed tapered I-beams before, but God guided us and they turned out beautifully. Ublan Viterbo and Bobby Burgos, two skilled young men in our church, did most of the welding. I laid out the design on the ground and they followed it precisely.

When it became time to raise the first truss into position, I went to the District Engineer's office to see if we could rent the only crane in the whole province for the job. The engineer informed me that the crane was in use, but he did say that they would do the job if we were willing to pay the price he quoted. We could not afford

Church construction

his price so I went back to talk over the situation with our crew. Domingo Absolon, our oldest and most experienced carpenter, assured me that we could lift the trusses ourselves. Following his suggestions, I borrowed two chain hoists and some heavy-duty pulleys to be used as a block and tackle. I then bought a long, new, one-inch thick nylon rope to be used in the block and tackle. We fastened the block and tackle to a steel ring embedded in the peak of the already finished concrete wall and hooked the other end of the rope to the Ford Fierra. We then built tripods from which to hang the chain blocks so they could assist in the lift about half way out from the peak on either side.

When everything was ready, I impressed upon everyone the necessity of our working in unison. I did my best to explain to the driver of the Fierra that he must watch me and not stop until I told him to. Everything went well until the truss was about halfway up. Then everything went wrong! The driver stopped to see how things were going. This placed undue stress on the other components. One chain block blew apart! A rope came untied and everything came crashing down. It was like an earthquake when the truss hit the ground! Bobby Burgos was almost hit by the truss but fortunately, everyone was able to get out of the way.

160

What went wrong? Several things. The one chain block, which I had been told had a two-ton capacity, was actually a half ton chain block. Domingo, who is a master at tying ropes, had tied the rope that came untied. Why it came untied I do not know. This, plus the fact that the driver stopped, added up to a near catastrophe. Praise God for His protection!

When we examined the truss, we found that it had not been damaged at all. It wasn't even twisted! I decided to try once again to get the crane. I went to the engineer's office and accused the District Engineer of trying to kill one of our men.

"What are you talking about?" he asked.

"Well, you wouldn't give us a decent price on the crane so we tried to lift a truss by ourselves and someone almost got killed!" I answered in an accusing fashion.

"What is it you want?" asked the engineer.

"I want you to lift the trusses for one-half the price you quoted me," I answered.

"Oh, okay," he answered with a sigh. "When do you want us to lift the first one?"

"Tomorrow at 7:00 a.m."

The next morning, the crane was there, and we quickly lifted the first heavy truss into position and bolted on several steel purlins on each side to hold it in place. The crane then left while we finished bolting and welding everything in place. This procedure was repeated for five days until all trusses were in place. As I sighted down the row of trusses, I was very pleased that they were in perfect alignment with each other and also with the slant on the end wall!

During the construction, I felt a good deal of stress wondering if the money would come in to complete the job. I guess I lacked real faith. We had started the building with very little money in hand. Little by little, funds came in. The local members gave as much as they could. The College Avenue Church came through with their promised $25,000. My cousin and her husband gave $5,000, and several others contributed smaller amounts. Finally, the Grace Church Edina came through with $15,000. When this amount was depleted, I called Kenny Kenerud to ask about the remaining portion of their faith promise. He informed me that, for some reason, their faith promise income had been coming in very slowly that year. "God has the money," he stated, "but as of now, we don't." He encouraged us to pray.

Then came the week when a decision had to be made. We had only a small amount of money left. What should we do? I felt that if we ended up with an unfinished building, it would be an embarrassment to us and to God. The whole community, yes, the whole province, was watching our construction. I talked the situation over with Elenor. I explained that we could eliminate the last eighteen-foot span facing the street. This would mean no offices, nursery, or balcony, but the public would not know that the plans had been changed, and neither God nor we would be embarrassed. We would still have the largest Protestant church in the whole region and it would be beautiful. I decided to call a meeting of the building committee for Friday evening at 5:00 to discuss this possibility.

Thursday night was a rough night for me as I tossed and turned in my bed. Friday was the same. I just didn't know what to do. Finally at 3:00 on Friday afternoon, I asked Pastor Martinez to hop on his motorcycle and inform all members of the building committee that I had cancelled the meeting. I just couldn't face the committee and show such lack of faith. God had been faithful thus far. Certainly, He wouldn't let us down now.

That night I struggled with God. I pleaded with Him to show us what He wanted us to do. It was His church. He should make the decision. What a thrill it was the very next morning to receive a letter from Grace Church Edina containing a check for $20,000! The exact amount needed to finish the building! What a wonderful God we have! How we rejoiced! How ashamed I was that I had doubted His provision.

The remainder of the construction went smoothly. God provided good workmen—all of them from Masbate. We used the best available materials throughout the building. We hired people to gather pebbles from the beaches of Ticao Island and covered all of the floors and some of the walls with pebbles embedded in the concrete (wash-out). Other sections of the walls were covered with a plaster coat composed mainly of tiny seashells, which we gathered from a small island near Milagros. These shells were mixed with Portland cement at a ratio of one part cement to four parts seashells. After the plaster had dried for a few hours, we used hatchets to chip away the smooth outer surface. This left a rough sparkling finish that is very beautiful. Both of these coverings require no upkeep other than occasionally cleaning off the moss and mildew, which sometimes develops in the shaded exterior areas.

Fortunately, I had signed a contract with the Philippine Steel Corporation to supply galvanized corrugated steel sheeting for the roof, with an additional five coats of acrylic golden colored paint. Since the factory they were building to manufacture this product was not finished by the delivery date stated in the contract, they were forced to give us imported sheets from Australia at the same price. We tried to construct everything in such a way that would require very minimal upkeep.

In addition to the actual building, we also built our own office and platform furniture. We constructed sixty-four pews using beautiful two-inch thick mahogany. We decided to use the pews from the old church in the balcony.

When the building was finished, we poured concrete sidewalks and driveways, as well as a concrete basketball court located between the old and the new church buildings.

On June 6, 1982, we held our first service in the new building. What a thrill! Everything was so beautiful! Elenor enjoyed playing the new electric organ we had purchased with funds given in memory of my mother.

The following Sunday, we held a baptismal service using the new baptistery on the right hand side

Masbate Baptist Church

of the platform. It was constructed in such a way that those being baptized enter the water from stairs in the counseling room and only become visible to the audience after they are in the water. This makes it possible for the baptismal service to be part of the worship service without any interruption. What a thrill to hear all twenty-seven candidates give testimonies telling of their new lives in Jesus Christ.

The dedication of the new building was on June 20, 1982. It was a great day with over 1,100 people present. A representative of the Provincial Governor, the Provincial Commander, the Municipal Mayor, as well as Rev. Joel Villamor the

General Secretary of the Baptist Conference of the Philippines were all present and brought greetings. Rev. Gonzalo Olojan, the pastor of the First Baptist Church of Cebu City, brought the main message. His name was well known in Masbate because we usually used at least two of his Cebuano messages each week on our "Voice of Truth" radio broadcast. A fifteen-member Wooddale Action Corps from Wooddale Church of Eden Prairie, MN was also present and contributed puppet shows and special music throughout the day.

I also brought a short message introducing our church building to the many visitors who were really looking around to see what a Protestant church looked like on the inside. I explained that we worshiped a living Savior and therefore there was no image attached to the lighted cross in the front of our church. I pointed to the baptistery

Audience in Masbate
Baptist Church

and explained why we needed "much water" to properly symbolize the true meaning of baptism and to obey the command of Jesus Christ to be immersed in water. I explained that the Bible and its teachings must always be central in our worship and for that reason the pulpit was in the center of the platform.

The program was quite long, but no one complained, as all knew that a feast would follow. We had butchered two cows, eight pigs, fifty-one chickens, and three goats. I don't remember how many sacks of rice were cooked, but no one went away hungry.

The celebration continued throughout the day and into the evening on Sunday. Besides presenting musical numbers and puppet shows, the Wooddale Action Corps basketball team played several games against local teams. There were formal services both Sunday and Monday evenings. Rev. Olojan was the speaker.

The following Sunday, I was the speaker. It rained that morning and attendance was not as high, but God was present. There were nine people who came forward to accept Jesus Christ as their personal Savior. That afternoon, two more accepted Him in a Bible study that I conducted.

God is so good! Praise His wonderful name!

Thirty-Four

A MOTHER SUPERIOR
FINDS THE LORD

On Christmas Eve 1983, Elenor and I were sitting in our living room relaxing after the usual activities of the Christmas season. At about eight o'clock we were startled by a knock on our door. When I opened the door I was surprised to see two women standing there. The first I recognized as Mrs. Maristela, a member of our church; the other I did not recognize, though she obviously knew me.

"Reverend, I found the Lord!" she blurted out.

"You did! Come on in and tell me about it."

I then realized that it was Sister Sylvia Martinez, the Mother Superior, who had served in the neighboring town of Mobo. She is a relative of both Pastor Martinez and Mrs. Maristela.

After being seated, she told the amazing story of her seven-year pilgrimage of coming to the light. She was born in Batuan, Ticao, Masbate, and had dedicated her life to become a nun in the Catholic Church. While serving as a nun for sixteen years, she organized her own sisterhood in Mobo, Masbate. Later, she was transferred to Manila where she had held several important positions in the Catholic Church. The last of these was to serve as one of two representatives

Sister Sylvia

of the Catholic Church on the committee working with the Philippine Bible Society in the production of a Common Bible to be used by both Catholics and Protestants.

When in Masbate, she had listened to our "Voice of Truth" radio broadcast and had also been witnessed to by some of our members. She told of how the Lord continued to speak to her and how she eventually found salvation and peace in Jesus Christ. She told, in great detail, an amazing story of her attempts to get out of the Catholic Church, and the intrigues of several priests to prevent this from happening.

"Now I have come home to Masbate to win my province-mates to the Lord," she stated with what appeared to be sincere enthusiasm.

After hearing her story, I told her that, if she wanted to give her testimony publicly in Masbate, she could use the platform of our church. She readily agreed. I then asked her if she had gone home to Batuan to tell her family of her experience.

"Not yet," she answered.

"Don't you think you ought to go home and tell them first?" I asked.

"Okay, I'll go home tomorrow, but I'll be back on Sunday. I'll attend your services on Sunday morning and then on Sunday evening I'll give my testimony in your church."

I was not sure if she would be back, but on Sunday morning, she was there and was determined to give her public testimony. The news spread quickly and that night, the Masbate Baptist Church was packed.

After a short introduction, I gave her the platform. She seemed very nervous. I didn't realize at the time that several of the men in the back row were Catholic priests in street clothes. Her testimony was fascinating as she recited her experiences—part of which included some of the sordid details of incidents with Catholic priests. She is a very gifted speaker, and the audience sat in rapt attention.

When her testimony was over, I called several of the leaders of our church into my office.

"Is she telling the truth?" I asked.

In unison, they answered, "Yes, she is telling the truth."

"If she is, she's in danger. What do you think we ought to do to help her?" I asked.

As we discussed her situation, the leaders of the church felt limited in what they could do because of a lack of funds.

"Do you think she could help us with the translation of the Bible into Masbatiño?" I asked.

"Yes, she would be great," they answered, "but where would we get the money to pay her salary?"

"If I could find the necessary funds, do you think it would be a good idea?" I asked. All agreed it would.

"Where would she live?" I asked.

"She can stay at my house," offered Mr. Tusing. Mr. Tusing had formerly been the President of the Holy Name Society in the Catholic Church.

After people had gone home, I talked further with Sister Sylvia and invited her to come to my office the following morning. When she arrived, I talked with her about the great need for a Masbatiño New Testament and of our plan to produce one. I asked her if she would like to work with us in producing it.

"Yes, of course. I would love to," was her immediate response.

When I told her about Mr. Tusing's offer to stay in his house, she wanted to go for a firsthand look at the situation. As Mr. Tusing showed her an available room in his beautiful house, I noticed that she wasn't paying much attention to the house. She was more interested in the height of the concrete fence surrounding it. It was obvious that she was afraid for her life.

During the next few weeks, she came regularly to our office and began working with us. Gradually, she felt more and more at ease and, little by little. she shared more of her experiences in working with morally degraded priests.

Then one day, she failed to appear at the office. No one seemed to know where she had gone or what had happened to her. We were all concerned, but later learned through the grapevine that she had gone to Manila. We wondered what was up.

About a week or ten days later, there was a knock on my office door. When I called "Come in," there was Sister Sylvia.

"May I speak with you alone?" she asked.

"Of course," I answered. "Close the door behind you."

She then explained that she had gotten an emergency call from her sister in Manila, who was in the hospital. Sylvia rushed to Manila immediately without even taking the time to notify us. When she arrived at the Makati Medical Center, she found her sister in serious condition. She had stayed in the hospital with her until she improved.

Sylvia then related that while she was in the hospital, Monsignor Villaroya, the parish priest from the St. Anthony Cathedral in Masbate, also came to visit her sister. While he was there, he insisted that Sister Sylvia have a medical examination.

"I didn't want to have a medical examination, but he kept insisting," she said. "When I finally agreed they discovered that I am pregnant!"

"Pregnant! How did that happen?" I asked.

"Well, when I came to see you that first time on Christmas Eve, what you did not know was that I had traveled all the previous night by bus down the south road from Manila to Bulan and then taken the launch to Masbate. When I left your house, I had no place to go but back to my old room in the Convent. When I reached my room, I was so exhausted that I just flopped down on my bed and fell asleep. In the middle of the night, the Monsignor came in through the unlocked door and I was not able to resist his wishes."

Sylvia had previously mentioned the Monsignor several times as she related her stories to me. She had explained that he was very close to her family. Sylvia's sister worked as a secretary in the cathedral and her mother was also close to this priest. He and Sylvia were in several business transactions together in raising funds. She explained that, as a Mother Superior, it was her responsibility to finance all of the operations of her convent.

"Do you love him?" I asked.

"No! I am afraid of him! When he found out I was pregnant he wanted me to have an abortion. When I refused, he offered to rent an apartment for me in Manila and supply a maid to take care of me. He told me that that is what the other priests from Masbate had done in similar situations. Reverend, I'm afraid to accept his offer. He may have my food poisoned!"

I decided to have a talk with Monsignor Villaroya. When I approached him at the cathedral, I asked him if I could have a private talk with him. He agreed to come to our house that night at 7:00.

When he arrived, we went into our living room and had a long private talk together. He was very open with me and readily admitted that he was the father of the unborn child. I actually did not spend much time talking about Sylvia's situation that evening. I talked about his situation as a sinner before God. I did my best to explain the Biblical way to find forgiveness and new life in Jesus Christ. After hours of discussing his situation, I finally came to the point of asking him to confess his sins to Jesus Christ and to surrender to Him as his Lord and Savior. At first I thought he was going to do it, but then he looked up and said, "I can't do it now."

"Why not?" I asked. "The Bible says that today is the accepted time."

"No," he said, "I must pay for my sins first."

"If you want to pay for your sins—that means you will go to hell. You'll be separated from God! Why not accept the payment Christ made on your behalf?"

I continued to struggle with him and pray for him, but to no avail. He just kept repeating, "I have to pay for my sins first."

At about eleven o'clock that evening, he excused himself and we parted. He went away a very heavily burdened man. I heard a few days later that he had left for the United States.

During the next few days, Sylvia told me many stories that I could hardly believe. She told of how the Rector of Santa Thomas University had worked with her on the Common Bible project. He had gone to her Bishop and had her transferred, against her will, to his office.

She told many almost unbelievable stories of what happened next. Various attempts were made to seduce her into immorality. Her superior was a very degenerate person and attempted many things, which cannot be repeated in this story. One time, he even went to the point of checking the two of them into a hotel in Davao City as husband and wife when they went there, supposedly, for a Bible conference.

She told of one afternoon, while she was taking a bath in the first floor bathroom of her convent in Manila, a limousine had pulled up and goons had jumped out and grabbed her naked out of the shower. They threw a towel around her and rushed her off to a hospital, where the Rector had her checked in as his maid who had gone crazy. He had her roped to a bed and repeatedly injected with Demerol.

"I pretended that I was crazy," she said. "They gave me a tin can to urinate in—so I saved my urine and threw it at anyone who came near me." The rector had her room guarded twenty-four hours a day—often he was the guard.

Fortunately, a doctor, whose son Sylvia had previously helped get off drugs, passed by the door of her room and recognized Sylvia.

"What are you doing here?" he asked. "What has happened to you?"

Sylvia quickly told him what had happened and asked him to inform her sister who worked for the NBI, the Phlippine equivalent of the FBI. Her sister went to the movie industry and got a specialist in disguise to help. He and another person went to the hospital and while one distracted the Rector, the other one cut Sylvia's ropes, pulled a wig over her head, and threw a robe around her, instructing her to put her head on his shoulder as though they were lovers. They walked out right in front of the Rector without him recognizing Sylvia.

Sylvia told me that she then went to her Bishop and told him what had happened. He just patted her on the shoulder and said, "Sylvia, you love your church. Now you must suffer for your church." She was ordered not to tell any one what happened.

Sylvia then decided to go home to Masbate and to get help from friends and relatives. She first went to Dr. Santiago, who was a graduate of Santa Thomas University, and asked him to certify that her arms had rope burns on them and that she had been successively injected with Demerol. He told her that he could see marks on her arms but he could not certify what had caused the marks.

Upon getting no help from Dr. Santiago, Sylvia then went to the Governor for help. After hearing her story, the Governor's only advice was "Wipe him out! I'll loan you some of my goons."

According to Sylvia, the arrangements were made and they agreed to do the job for 10,000 pesos. When Sylvia had raised the amount, she went to the agreed upon meeting place in Manila to deliver the cash. When she got there, she gave the money to the goons but then called off the job. She couldn't go through with it.

"That was the night that I took the long bus and launch trip to Masbate and came to your house. You had no idea what I had just gone through."

"No, I certainly did not."

I called John Fast, one of our missionaries in Manila who had recently arrived in the Philippines. When he heard the story, he invited Sylvia to come to Manila and live with them and teach them the Tagalog dialect.

As I reviewed in my mind the many stories Sylvia told (I have only included a few of them here), I sometimes wondered if all of them could possibly be true. It seemed impossible that leaders of a church could stoop so low as to do the things she described. I wanted to get the opinion of someone who knew what was really going on in the Catholic Church.

One day, when I was in Manila, I took Sylvia to the home of Rev. Anthony Pezzotta, a missionary who was serving with the Conservative Baptists. Antonio was born in Bergamo, Italy. He studied fifteen years in Roman Catholic seminaries of the Salesians of Don Bosco in Italy, England, Spain and Germany. He was ordained a Catholic priest on February 11, 1961. When he came to the Philippines, he was made a director of schools and seminaries, as well as a rector of local Salesian communities (1964–1974). On February 26, 1974, after studying the Scriptures on his own and through the testimony of Rev. Ernesto Montealegre, a Filipino Baptist pastor, Tony (as he likes to be called) trusted Christ alone as Savior and Lord and left the Catholic Church. Later, he went to the states, and after studying at Denver Seminary, was appointed by the Conservative Baptists as a missionary to the Philippines.

When we arrived at the home of Rev. Pezzotta, I asked Sylvia to tell her life story to Tony. When she finished, I asked Tony to step outside.

"Is she telling the truth?" I asked. "Can these stories possibly be true?"

"Of course they are true," Tony stated emphatically. He indicated that he could tell many more.

When I first went to the Philippines as a missionary, I purchased several books from Christ's mission in New York. This mission was composed of former priests and nuns. As I read their books and publications, I could hardly believe the stories they recorded. Now after spending almost forty years in the Philippines, I can believe almost anything.

In recent years, the newspapers here in the United States have been filled with similar stories. The Catholic Church in some areas, is almost bankrupt as a result of large penalties imposed upon the Church by the courts because of the immoral actions of many priests. I hope and pray that this will lead to true repentance on the part of the Catholic Church and to a turning from the many immoral practices that for years have been kept secret but are now coming into the open. We need to pray that, in the process, many of these leaders will come to the light and find new life in Jesus Christ as Tony and Sister Sylvia have.

Thirty-Five

A TRAGIC MURDER

I n 1936, a very tragic murder occurred in Masbate. Tenten, the daughter of my good friend, Dr. Pablo Santa Cruz, discovered that her husband was having an affair with a lady worker of the Catholic Church, who was also their house guest. During an argument, Tenten was so distraught that she grabbed her husband's gun and fatally shot him. Her husband was the son of a prominent doctor in Milagros with whom I had been having Bible studies. Tenten immediately surrendered to the authorities and was detained at the constabulary police compound.

Several days after the shooting, Pablo came to my house requesting me to go with him to Milagros to try to convince Dr. De Castro, the father of the deceased, not to press charges. Pablo explained that his daughter, Tenten, had lived a very difficult life and had previously been shot at sev-

Visiting Dr. Santa Cruz

eral times by her husband—once hitting the chair on which she was sitting and once hitting her Bible. In fact, it was his gun that she had grabbed from his hands to shoot him. Pablo said he had tried everything to convince Dr.

De Castro not to press charges against his daughter but to no avail. He had even taken the Roman Catholic Bishop with him but, again, Dr. De Castro would not listen.

He insisted that he would file charges against Tenten, his daughter-in-law.

"You are my only hope. Maybe he will listen to you," pleaded Pablo with tears running down his cheeks.

I did not know what to do. I did not want to become involved. I did not want to be seen as someone seeking to obstruct justice. "And yet," I wondered, "what is justice in this case?" I knew that if Tenten were consigned to a Philippine penitentiary it would be hell on earth. I also thought of her young children and what would happen to them. I knew she was no danger to society, and I knew that her husband had often mistreated and threatened her with his gun. After much pleading from Pablo, I finally decided to go.

When we arrived at the De Castro home, we found a very tense situation. Dr. De Castro was obviously grieving over what had happened to his son and determined for revenge. I talked with him very calmly and explained the situation as I saw it.

"We cannot undo what has been done. We must go on. We must seek the best solution for the family—especially the children. What will happen to your grandchildren if their mother is put in jail?"

"But she killed my son! She must be punished!"

"Yes, she killed your son. What she did was wrong, but we cannot change that," I answered. "Remember, however, that your son was far from perfect. Are you aware of the fact that he, at several times, shot at your daughter-in-law? I have seen the hole shot in her Bible. I have seen the mark left by the bullet on her chair. If you go to court, these details will be brought out. Will they not bring great shame to your family? I believe the wisest thing for you two grieving parents is to work out some amicable settlement without going to the courts. This is my frank advice to both of you."

I could see that Dr. De Castro was getting the point of what I was saying. After a time, he got up and walked out of the room. This left Pablo and me alone, wondering what would happen. When he returned, he looked at both of us and said, "All right, I will do as you have advised. If Tenten and her father will agree to the following stipulations, I will not file charges." He had made a list.

After looking over the stipulations, which mostly had to do with the guardianship of the children and the management of properties, Pablo accepted the proposal. We shook hands and the deal was closed.

It might be well for me to point out that in the Philippines, at that time, the government prosecutors did not usually prosecute a murder within a family unless someone pressed charges. I have known of three cases where a father shot his own son and no charges were pressed.

My involvement in this matter was a very delicate issue. It could have backfired on me and brought harm to our cause. As it turned out, I believe I gained great respect from both of these prominent families, and I am happy to say that I was later able to lead Tenten to the Lord. One of her daughters also accepted the Lord and was later married to one of the members of our church. Though Dr. De Castro also professed to accept the Lord, there has never been clear evidence that his decision was real. Tenten is still a member of the Catholic Church and is seeking to win her friends to the Lord. She often comes to our church.

With Tenten

Thirty-Six

A WEALTHY RANCHER SEARCHES FOR PEACE

Aroroy, Masbate is a gold mining town. Before World War II, it had the largest gold mine in the Orient. One of our Bible College graduates named Ricardo Azares felt led by the Lord to start a church there. The Masbate Baptist Church agreed to support him. Ricardo was able to make many contacts with professional people who were community leaders and several were converted. Several times, he asked me to come and speak at their Sunday services.

During one of these visits, Rick and I made a visit to the home of "Baby" Dela Fuente, an old friend of mine. I had known Baby for many years and had previously shared the gospel with him. He had even once made a profession of salvation.

One day during my visit to Aroroy, he asked me to stay in his home overnight. I agreed and we talked way into the night. By this time, Baby had become the wealthiest man in the whole area. The extent of his wealth was indicated by the fact that he had just negotiated a loan of 230 million pesos for the expansion of his business.

As we talked on, I tried to shift the conversation to spiritual matters. As I did, he bluntly stated: "God would not have me. I am too great of a sinner."

"Jesus Christ came to save sinners," I explained.

"Yes, but not as bad as I am."

"Any sin can be forgiven if it is repented of and if we come to faith in Jesus Christ," I explained.

He then proceeded to explain what he considered to be his unforgivable sin. He owned a very large cattle ranch and he told of how his cattle had been continually stolen by a notorious group of rustlers. He had often reported this matter to the authorities but no action had been taken. In desperation, he eventually hired someone to eliminate the rustlers. The rustlers were later found dead. The people in the whole area rejoiced that their problem had finally been solved.

Baby, however, had a guilty conscience for what he had done. I told him that the early ranchers in the United States had often faced the same problem and had solved it in similar ways. I told him that I was not there to judge him but to point him to someone who could forgive any and all sins.

Baby bowed his head and, once again, prayed the sinner's prayer. Since that time, he has sometimes come to our services both in Aroroy and Masbate City, but as of now I am not sure where he really stands.

Aroroy Baptist Church

Tony Aplacador followed Ricardo as the pastor of the Aroroy Church. After being on the job for several months, Tony came to me explaining that he felt it was essential for the growth of the church that they get their own property and put up a permanent church building. I encouraged him to look for a good church site. Several times, he came to Masbate to inform me that he had found an available lot. When I surveyed these proposed sites, I found them to be located either on the very edge of town or in some other poor location.

After I had rejected several sites, Tony became very frustrated with me. When I would ask him if he thought God would want His church in any of those locations, he would answer in the negative. When I asked about some better site, he would always answer, "We could never afford that lot." To this I would usually answer by pointing to the sky and saying, "Talk to the owner."

I wanted him to realize that God is the owner of the whole town of Aroroy and that, at His time, He would give us a good location.

Then one day, while I was in the terminal building of the airport in Masbate, my old friend, Baby Dela Fuente, saw me and came over to greet me. It always amazed me that childhood nicknames often continued to be used even for adults.

"I understand you are looking for a lot on which to build a church in Aroroy," he stated. "Have you found one yet?"

"Yes, we are and no, we haven't," I answered. "Do you know of any good lot that is available?"

"Yes, I know of a very beautiful lot," Baby answered.

"Where?" I asked.

"That knoll right next to the elementary school buildings."

"Oh that," I answered. "I doubt that we would be able to afford that. By the way, who owns it?"

"I do and it's not for sale," answered Baby. "However, if you will have a Deed of Donation made out, I will sign it."

"Are you kidding?" I asked.

"No, I'm not kidding. Just go and look at it and if you think it is a good location for a church, I will give it to you."

I could hardly believe my ears! I believed, however, that Baby was sincere, so I went to Aroroy to examine the site. It turned out to be the choicest, most visible lot in the whole town. It contained about 7,000 square meters—the largest of any of our church sites.

The next time I saw Baby, I commented on what a beautiful lot it was. "Then you better come to my house in Manila for a meal and we will talk to Sonya about it," was Baby's immediate response. Sonya, his wife, was a leader in the Catholic Church, and I realized that perhaps she was opposed to Baby's commitment. We set a date, and Elenor and I made plans to go to Manila.

When we arrived at the Dela Fuente residence in one of the suburbs of Manila, we were received very cordially. They had prepared a sumptuous meal for us and we enjoyed our fellowship with them. After the meal, Baby just blurted out, "Sonya, Rev. Varberg wants our lot in Aroroy as a site for their church. What do you think?"

Sonya looked at me for a while and then asked, "Rev. Varberg, you know that I am a leader in the Catholic Church. What do you think my fellow Catholics would say if we gave the lot to you for a Baptist Church?"

"I think they would be very disappointed and perhaps even angry with you," I answered honestly.

There was silence for a while and then Sonya continued. "Will you promise that if we give the lot to your church you will not attempt to proselyte any of our Roman Catholic members?"

I thought for a moment and decided that I would answer frankly and honestly. "Sonya," I said, "I promise that I will try my best to proselyte all of your members—including you."

Sonya looked shocked by my frankness and honesty. I wondered what would happen. The conversation shifted to other topics as the evening wore on and I wondered if we had lost our chance to obtain the best lot in Aroroy.

After a while Baby again brought up the subject. "Sonya, Rev. Varberg needs our answer. What do you think?"

After some hesitation, Sonya just blurted out: "Progress must go on. Give him the lot."

I could hardly believe my ears! Was Sonya really agreeing to the donation?

Though Sonya only reluctantly agreed, she did sign the donation papers. Today, the Aroroy Church has the largest lot of any of our churches and since it is located on a knoll overlooking the town, it is one of the most visible. It seems that the apostle Paul had many similar experiences when he wrote: "Now to him who is able to do immeasurably more than all we ask or imagine, according to his power that is at work within us, to him be glory in the church and in Christ Jesus throughout all generations, for ever and ever!" (Eph. 3:20-21)

Thirty-Seven

GOD STRETCHES MY FAITH BUT NOT HIS RESOURCES

The situation of our church plant in Bulan became critical when the owner of the old post office, where the church was meeting, gave notice that the church would have to vacate the building. The Pastor of the church in Bulan was Alex Fontilar. Shortly after receiving this notice, Pastor Fontilar came to Masbate to inform me of the situation, I encouraged him to search for a good lot where we could build our own church building.

One day, he found a site that he thought was good and came to Masbate requesting that I come and examine it. We loaded my motorcycle onto the *Matea*, a launch that goes to Bulan several times a week, and took the five-hour trip to Bulan. When Alex showed me the proposed site, I was disappointed. It was in a squatter area near the pier. When I met with the owner and examined the papers, I found that there was no clear title of ownership. The person claiming ownership was also asking an exorbitant price. I suggested to Alex that we ride around the town and look for a better site. Due to the fact that Bulan has a good pier, it is the key commercial center of the southern Bicol region. Though we found no available lots that day, I felt sure that a better lot would soon become available if Alex kept his eyes and ears open. I encouraged him to look for the best lot in town and, pointing towards the sky, suggested he talk with the owner.

Several weeks later, Alex came back to Masbate all excited. He wanted me to come immediately, as the owner of a very beautiful lot wanted to leave for the states. Since the owner was lacking money, he agreed to sell his lot if we could pay him in cash immediately. The next day, I again took the launch to Bulan. This time, Alex was right. It was a beautiful, centrally located lot with a hollow block fence surrounding it. It also had a clear title. The only problem was that he wanted one million pesos for the lot. I didn't know what to do. We had never paid that much for a lot before. When I inquired around town, however, I discovered that it was a fair price for that quality of lot in Bulan.

I decided to go home and ask the advice of the Masbate Baptist Church leadership. When I described the situation, they asked me if we had one million pesos available. I told them that if we used all of the funds from every account and sold a small lot that we were not using in Masbate, we might be able to reach that amount. After many more questions, they advised me to go back to Bulan and look at the lot one more time. "Then," they instructed, "make whatever decision you feel God would have you make."

That night, I picked up a book and read the story of a man who was going out at night with his car. When he turned on his headlights, his passenger told him to stop.

"Why?" asked the driver.

"Because your lights are too dim; they only reach to the gate."

"Don't worry," answered the driver. "When the car goes forward, so will the lights."

I took that as a sign from God that I should go forward in faith. After all, I had previously made a decision to never let the lack of funds hinder me from doing what I believed God wanted me to do. Though God had proven Himself faithful in many previous instances, I must admit, however, that as I again boarded the launch headed for Bulan, I felt a heavy load on my shoulders. I hated to spend practically every centavo we had for just one lot. On the other hand, we had asked the Lord to give us the best lot in Bulan and now it was being offered to us. Should we not then proceed?

When I reached Bulan, Alex and I again went to the site. We prayed and asked God for guidance. Then, we went to the home of the owner. After discussing various details with him, I decided to proceed with the purchase. I had brought only enough money to make a down payment, as I expected the owner would agree to give us several days to complete the payment.

As I again boarded the launch for the long trip back to Masbate, I didn't know whether to be happy or sad. I realized that many other programs would have to be either delayed or cancelled, unless God somehow miraculously supplied additional funds.

As I pondered what to do, I remembered that we had received a letter in December from a member of Grace Church Edina named Allen Wehr. He is a friend of Ray Becker, who had financed most of the construction of the Mandaon Church. After talking with Ray, Allen had written to us asking if we had any similar projects to which he could contribute. I had answered in a rather indefinite way. I told him that I was not sure how much longer we would be in the Philippines as we were nearing retirement. I did tell him of the need for several church sites in the county seats of Bulan, Irosin, and San Francisco. I explained how the skyrocketing prices hindered our purchase of lots in these areas. I also told him that we had committed the matter to the Lord and were waiting on the Lord to supply the funds if He wanted us to proceed.

Before leaving for Bulan, I asked Elenor to write a follow-up letter to Allen and his wife Judy updating them on what had just taken place. I asked her to explain how I had used funds from several accounts to complete the payment and that if these funds were not replaced, our whole program would be jeopardized. I did not know what their reaction would be, but I prayed that somehow they would be able to help.

When I reached Bulan to complete the payment everything went smoothly. I felt glad that I was able to make the full payment even though it meant borrowing money from several accounts. As I made the long five-hour trip back to Masbate with the title of the property in my briefcase, I rejoiced but with a troubled mind. I must admit that sometimes my faith is not as strong as it should be. I began to wonder what negative results would occur in our whole program because of this very expensive purchase.

When I reached Masbate, Noe, the foreman of our construction crew, handed me a letter. It stated that the construction of the San Jacinto church was almost finished. He asked for instructions as to where the the construction crew should go from there.

Bulan Bible Community Church

That night, I didn't sleep very well as I realized that I would have to bring the crew back to Masbate and lay them off, unless God somehow supplied unexpected funds.

The next morning, I loaded my motorcycle into an outrigger canoe headed for Lagundi, on Ticao Island. From there, I rode about one hour to San Jacinto. When I arrived at the church site, the crew was packing up the equipment. As I examined the buildings, I saw that they had done an excellent job. I complimented the crew and took a picture of the buildings. I then sat down on a log. Noe came over and asked where they would go next.

"I don't know," I answered.

"What do you mean you don't know?

"I just spent all of our money buying a lot in Bulan."

Noe looked at me with a strange somewhat shocked look on his face. I put my head in my hands and asked God what to do. Finally, I looked up and told Noe to ship the equipment to Bulan and store it on the lot I had just purchased. I instructed him to ask Pastor Alex to get someone to guard the equipment and then bring the crew home to Masbate.

My trip back to Masbate that night seemed very long. I knew I had purchased an excellent lot, but the future seemed so uncertain. What would the draining of all of our funds do to our whole program? It seemed everything was up in the air.

That night, I prayed earnestly for God to clearly show me what to do. The next morning when I picked up our mail, I noticed a letter from a company in Minneapolis that I did not recognize.

"Do we have any unpaid bills in Minneapolis?" I asked Elenor.

"Not that I know of," she answered.

"Then what is this letter?" I asked as I opened the envelope. To my utter amazement, I read the following letter from Allen Wehr dated March 21, 1996, that he mailed in a company envelope.

Dick:

Judy and I have been praying and thinking about what the Lord would have us do since we received your first letter. And then we got the second letter dated 3/8/96.

The amount that we had confirmed in our minds before receiving your letter was $19,000. Your letter mentioned the $19,000 amount as what you had to pay for property in Bulan....interesting....I had sold some things and they exactly totaled $19,000 in preparation for what we might do.

I called Bob Ricker today and then further visited with Ron Larson. I am sending the BGC a check for $19,000 today. Ron assured me that the entire $19,000 would be forwarded to your account for this project. You can repay whatever accounts that that money was taken from to buy that piece of property (or whatever).

We are glad to partner with you and Elenor. May God continue to bless you and the ministry and give you direction in the next months as "work" changes a bit for you and your family.

In Christ,

Allen and Judy Wehr

I could hardly believe my eyes! Nineteen thousand dollars was the exact equivalent of one million pesos! It took several days for me to come back down to earth again. It seemed that I was in heaven! How I rejoiced that God had once again made Himself and His power real to me! How could I have ever doubted Him? I also realized that He had been preparing things ahead of time to bring about this wonderful conclusion.

> *"Before they call I will answer: while they are still speaking I will hear." (Isaiah 66:24)*

Thirty-Eight

72 BAPTIZED IN ONE SERVICE

During the early nineties, I was concerned that, though we were continuing to grow and plant new churches, some of our older churches (including the mother church of which I was the Senior Pastor) were not growing as rapidly as I felt they should. We prayed much and sought to find the answer. Then during a visit by Ron Larson and John Marrs, I was introduced to the *Purpose Driven Church*, a new book that had just been written by Rick Warren. After reading portions of John's copy, I immediately ordered several copies to be brought from the states by our daughter, Debra, who was planning to visit us.

This book was a tremendous help to us. We found that we had not clearly defined our purposes in several areas. This led to a reevaluation of our whole program, and by using some of the tools and strategies outlined by Rick Warren, we saw new life and a real surge of growth in the mother church. As daughter churches began to see what God was doing in the mother church, they too began to evaluate their programs.

Masbate Baptist Bible College

Soon, they began using the materials we were producing and this sparked a similar fire in their churches.

While this was going on, I began teaching *The Purpose Driven Church* as a subject at the Masbate Baptist Bible College (MBBC). As the students saw firsthand the results of this program in the mother church (MBC), they, too, began implementing the program in the churches where they had their weekend assignments.

Seventy-two baptized
in one day!

On September 15, 1996, we decided to do something special. We invited some of the neighboring daughter churches to join with us for a special day of celebration and fellowship at Bituon Beach. There was such great enthusiasm that we had a problem transporting so many people to the beach. We used all of the vehicles owned by our members, and we borrowed or rented other vehicles. It was quite a sight to see nine to ten large trucks, twelve jeepney-type vehicles, and many motorcycles overflowing with enthusiastic Baptists and their friends! There was wonderful music, and after I had given the morning message under the coconut trees at the beach, seventy-two new believers (all with white t-shirts) lined up to be baptized. I carried a portable megaphone and called off the names as six pastors each baptized twelve persons. Among those baptized were Noe, the foreman of our construction crew, and one of his daughters.

Another was Maricel Sulat, who was later to become our daughter-in-law. Forty-five of those baptized were from the Masbate Baptist Church. After

1,500 gather at Bituon Beach

188

the baptism, we all shared the food we each prepared and ate our fill. The afternoon was spent in various organized sports and fun games that involved young and old alike. Elenor and I won the "Eating the Apple On the String" contest. There were 1,510 people in attendance.

"To God be the glory, great things He has done!"